**For the first time—
bestselling human relations experts
JULIUS AND BARBARA FAST
explore the unconscious level
of speech communication.**

Did you really mean what you just said? Did you send out a secret message that belied your words? How can you know what other people are trying to tell you—or hide from you? How can you avoid misunderstanding, hurt and angry quarrels?

In this revolutionary book, the Fasts explain how the meaning of what you say is vitally affected by breath, pitch, word choice and stress, rhythm, tone, inflection, volume, melody, and even dialect.

They offer you a powerful new tool for communicating successfully in every area of your life and for realizing the potential your words sometimes hide!

Books by Julius Fast

Body Language
Talking Between the Lines (with Barbara Fast)

Published by POCKET BOOKS

TALKING BETWEEN THE LINES

HOW WE MEAN MORE THAN WE SAY

JULIUS
AND
BARBARA FAST

PUBLISHED BY POCKET BOOKS NEW YORK

ACKNOWLEDGMENT

Simon & Schuster: From *The Name Game* by Christopher P. Andersen Copyright © 1977 by Christopher P. Andersen. Reprinted by permission of Simon & Schuster, a Division of Gulf & Western Corporation.

POCKET BOOKS, a Simon & Schuster division of GULF & WESTERN CORPORATION
1230 Avenue of the Americas, New York, N.Y. 10020

Reprinted by arrangement with the Viking Press
Library of Congress Catalog Card Number: 79-716

ISBN: 0-671-83244-1

First Pocket Books printing December, 1980

10 9 8 7 6 5 4 3 2 1

For Jennifer, Melissa, Timothy, and Daniel—
who have taught us how to communicate

Contents

TALKING
BETWEEN THE LINES

INTRODUCTION

All of us speak in at least two languages. There is the language we are familiar with, our spoken words. But behind these words, within them and around them, are numerous meanings that do not exist in the words themselves. This is a metalanguage, another form of communication whose meaning sometimes strengthens and sometimes weakens or even contradicts the words we speak. It accompanies the spoken words, and it includes resonance, pitch, stress, melody, and volume as well as dialect, accent, and the emotional overlay we give to words—sarcasm, tenderness, irony.

Anthropologist Gregory Bateson first used the term metacommunication to mean communication about communication, any message about how people communicated. Virginia Satir, a psychiatric therapist and writer, took the term a step further and wrote, "Humans cannot communicate without at the same time metacommunicating."

In this book we have gone beyond Satir to elucidate all the areas of metacommunication, the new language, and explain how we use them to help our own communication and also to understand the communication of others. In other words, we want to explain *how* we talk to each other.

There are many frequencies on the metacommunication band. There is accent and idiom, for example. The same message given by a Northerner and a Southerner can have different meanings because of the overlay of a Southern accent or a Northern one or because of familiar words used in an unfamiliar context.

Jargon, in business, medicine, politics, and science, is another frequency on the metaband. What is incomprehensible jargon to the outsider is often clear and a useful shorthand to the insider. The pervasiveness of jargon in our society is startling. Even young people have their own jargon, which, among other uses, serves to exclude adults.

There is an erotic frequency band on the metalevel, and it sometimes depends on the choice of words, sometimes on a foreign accent, and sometimes on the situation in which a word is spoken.

A special metacommunication exists between the sexes. This includes the use of pitch, volume, and melody; the selection of words; and vocal aggressiveness or submission.

We all use metacommunication to play semantic games, for game playing and words are old friends, but we are not always aware of just what game is being played. We use word games to bolster our egos, and we also use them to hurt others—and ourselves.

Often we talk without listening simply to get our own viewpoint across. We forget that communication should be a two-way street, each person revealing to the other a part of his thoughts, emotions, and very identity.

In interpersonal relationships, we disclose a tremendous amount about ourselves through metacommunication. Understanding and using metaskills can strengthen your message and help you to relate better to your lover, your family, your friends, the people you work with, and even strangers.

1

The Meta Is the Message

A NEW SCIENCE

"When I use a word," Humpty Dumpty said in rather a scornful tone, "it means just what I choose it to mean—neither more nor less."
"The question is," said Alice, "whether you can make words mean so many things."
"The question is," said Humpty Dumpty, "which is to be master—that's all."

In *Through the Looking Glass,* it was Humpty-Dumpty who was master, and he was able to dominate the conversation with Alice. He made the words mean whatever he wanted them to, whether or not Alice made any sense out of them. There is a little of Alice and a little of Humpty Dumpty in all of us. Like Humpty, we are all capable of manipulating our words and their meanings, and like Alice, we are prone to moments of absolute confusion in conversation.

Most people believe that a word means precisely

what the dictionary defines it to be, neither more nor less. In fact the dictionary has always been a device to stabilize the language and incorporate certain constant truths about words, whether they are used in Oshkosh, San Francisco, or Baton Rouge. This is still often true for the written word, but when English or any other language is spoken, another dimension is added, and that dimension is *metacommunication*.

Metacommunication is a new science born out of a marriage between language and psychiatry. It suggests that there is more to the word than the word itself. The word we select is important, but the way the word is packaged is just as important, perhaps more so. How it is selected, how it is used, how it is pronounced, all the vocal extras that surround it can communicate more than the word does. They can emphasize it, diminish it, or even contradict it.

Communication is a two-way street. We not only send messages, we also receive them, and we interpret what we receive according to our own perception. We perceive not only the word but everything that intensifies and colors it, and this must include what we know of the speaker and the situation. There is a history behind every personal communication, and if you would understand metacommunication, you must be aware of that history.

Take, for example, a young couple, Bob and Amy, who have been working on a "meaningful relationship" for the past year—with little success. One day Bob comes home and finds Amy in the bedroom, surrounded by open dresser drawers and suitcases.

"What are you doing?" he asks.

"Packing. I'm splitting," Amy snaps, brushing her hair back and staring tightly around the room. "We're never going to make it."

"But why?"

"Why? Because you never hear what I say."

"Oh, I hear you loud and clear," Bob answers angrily. "I know what you mean."

"I told you last night," Amy says with mock patience, "I was perfectly willing to go to your mother's house for dinner, and what did you say? 'Don't do me any favors!' "

"When you say you're *perfectly willing,* I know what you're getting at. Sure, you're *perfectly willing* to go to my mother's, and you're *perfectly willing* to have sex, and you're *perfectly willing* to stay home this vacation—I know that *perfectly willing* routine!"

Amy snaps her suitcase shut without another word, and a potentially happy relationship is over before it was really given a chance.

Here are two young people who have a lot in common, except for one thing—the ability to communicate honestly. Their words mean one thing. How they use those words means another. They are communicating on many different levels. Both are sending out emotional signals which reveal, in an unconscious way, more than they are willing to admit.

The pitch of the voice, the volume, stress, intonation, accent, intensity, and emotion—even the words we choose give a meaning beyond the words themselves. A word is a word is a word—depending on who says it, how it's said, and how it's heard. Amy's *perfectly* is so loaded with emotion that it denies her willingness.

Like Amy and Bob, everyone uses metacommunication. Some of us know just how it works, and some of us don't. Some are naturals at it, while others must learn how to use that extra wavelength.

NOT WHAT YOU SAY, BUT THE WAY THAT YOU SAY IT

During the 1976 Presidential campaign, the late Dr. Margaret Mead, the grand lady of anthropology, advised Jimmy Carter to concentrate on style rather than content. Once he was in office, one of Carter's advisors said very much the same thing. "The important factor is not what the President says, but how he says it."

This comes as no shock to those of us who watch and listen to politicians. We look for the extra touch of sincerity. As we listen, we ask ourselves, *Is he honest or is he talking out of both sides of his mouth? Can I trust him, or am I being conned?* We hear what he is saying, but we take in all the other signals, the metacommunication of *how* he is saying it, and we zero in on these. We have been fooled so often by the smooth approach, the humble stance, the aggressive voice, the soothing tone, that unconsciously we are alert to any betrayal of the spoken message with a metalie.

In *The Selling of the President* there is a memo cited from William Gavin, of Nixon's staff. In the memo Nixon is urged to remember the importance of "star style." Gavin defines this as "the aura that surrounds the man more than the man himself." He goes on to spell out the "extra dimension of inflection, the emotional overlay that the voice can give but the printed word cannot."

In advising Nixon how to act, Gavin gave a concise definition of one part of metacommunication, the *emotional overlay* that accompanies language, the smooth, harsh, gentle, raucous, pleading, sarcastic, wheedling, whining nuances that go with words, that shape them and change them, modify them and contradict them and add a different dimension to them.

Politicians depend on metacommunication for survival, and actors study it constantly to get their characters across on film, TV, and the stage. Salesmen should be aware of it, for the slightest jarring note in their voices can ruin a sale no matter how good a deal they offer. Con men, who make their living by playing on people's greed, are old pros at it.

The rest of us use metacommunication, but seldom with the awareness of politicians, actors, salesmen, and con men. A mother asks her teenage daughter, "Will you set the table?" and the daughter says, "All right." Consider this very simple exchange that goes on in so many homes every night. It can be a question and answer, a simple request and acceptance, a smiling, easygoing mother and a pleasant, cooperative daughter. But just vary the stress on the words the slightest bit.

"*Will* you set the table?"

"All *right*."

And you have set up a family conflict, a nagging mother and a recalcitrant daughter. You've started to blaze a trail into a Freudian jungle, all with two stresses.

A friend recently hired a young Englishwoman as a secretary. "She can't type for beans," he told us, "but she's worth every cent I pay her. That crazy English accent is what does it. The clients flip out over her. She just says, 'May I take a message?' and she generates more respect than any American secretary. She has class, and somehow that rubs off on the firm."

What my friend was saying is that an English accent carries a very special metacommunication here in the

States. Unconsciously we associate it with education, a higher social status, and culture. It signals *good breeding*.

By contrast, a French accent often signals sexuality. In the thirties and forties Charles Boyer became the nation's great lover less because of his acting ability than because of his sensuous, caressing voice, and today Catherine Deneuve sells automobiles and perfume with the same French caress.

GETTING TO KNOW YOU

A foreign accent can communicate sex, but other metasignals can do it too. Mae West managed it very nicely, in part by innuendo, but mostly by the extra sexual polish she gave to her words, the intimate intonation, tone, and stress behind them. Men and women both use tricks of intonation and modulation to signal sexual interest. Eavesdropping at a literary cocktail party in a big city can show us how it's done.

The room is pleasantly crowded, everyone packed against everyone else, and the hostess has long given up trying to introduce anyone. They're all bound to get to know each other soon enough.

Look at Jennifer. She turns to an interesting-looking man and says, "Hi! I'm Jennifer." Listen to the way she laces her introduction with metasignals. Her *hi* is soft, drawn out, and almost two syllables, and it ends on a slightly rising note. Her *Jennifer* slides down the scale, and is a warm announcement of her own identity. The total effect carries the metamessage *Aren't you lucky to meet me! I promise an exciting time if we get together*.

The man, with a pleased smile, says, "Well, hello!"

He slurs over the *well* and accents the second syllable of *hello*. He has received Jennifer's signal and returns one of his own.

But now listen to Cathy in another corner of the room. She too sees a man with promise and she says, "Hi! I'm Cathy." But unlike Jennifer's *hi*, Cathy's is definitely one syllable and swallowed before it's entirely out. Her *Cathy* is a straight statement of fact without much rise or fall to any part of it. What she says is true, but it signals nothing more than her name and promises nothing except, to a discerning ear, a touch of honesty. Her metasignals are restrained and forthright.

Fortunately, the man Cathy has singled out can't stand coyness. He responds to Cathy with "My name's Bob. Are you in publishing too?" They both avoid much of the sexual metagame, and they cut through to a quick understanding of each other. But they use metacommunication to do it.

Cathy and Jennifer used the metawavelengths fluently, and the men they met used them too. Where did they all learn it, and how? Where and when do any of us learn it? Some social scientists believe that it is programmed into us, strung on our genetic necklace along with the shade of our hair and the color of our eyes. They suggest that the newborn baby arrives with the ability to receive and send metasignals.

Other scientists feel that it is all learned, and that we start the learning process the moment we are born. In fact, some insist that we learn signals in the womb. Research suggests that an unborn baby responds to the ringing of a bell placed on his mother's stomach.

In any case, children all over the world know metacommunication before they know how to speak. They seem to absorb it from their parents or anyone else who cares for them. An American baby hears his father make soft, cooing sounds and he responds with gurgles of pleasure. No words are exchanged, but a message still goes back and forth.

Three thousand miles away an African father, squatting beside a mat where his baby son is lying, sends and receives the same messages, and still farther east, on a junk in Hong Kong's harbor, a Chinese father comforts his crying baby with the identical soothing sounds.

In each case the sounds of comfort and pleasure, the cooing and the response, are the same. They spell caring and comfort. If each father were to raise his voice, to shape his words harshly, and with anger, each baby would respond in the same way, with tears and wails.

In part, these first steps seem instinctive on both sides. All normal parents gurgle and coo at their babies, and all normal babies gurgle back. Musically, baby sounds are about six to eight half-tones in the mid-soprano range, plus a few high notes, but even with this limited range the baby can express his moods, communicate his needs, and react to his parents. He can coo softly when he's comfortable, cry in a hard and demanding way when he's uncomfortable, and, in general, experiment and play with sounds.

Very soon the child learns to link his mother's voice to food, warmth, and comfort, and by the time he is two or three months old, he has discovered the full power of his own metacommunication. He knows just which sound can produce Mother, food, dry diapers, soothing words, and comforting arms. He knows which sounds make Mother pick him up and which make her rock him to sleep. He begins to understand, too, that the same sounds which help him manipulate Mother also help him manipulate other people.

Gradually the baby's metasignals become differentiated. He learns to react to certain stimuli. Fear produces one kind of sound, anger another, love still another.

All of this takes place on an unconscious level, but very soon culture steps in. Studies have shown that while the mother and father both give early metasignals to the baby, the mother's signals are different, and the baby responds differently to each. Sexual differences take over. The boy baby is handled more roughly than the girl, and his response is rougher, the girl's gentler. We have the beginning of the aggressive boy and the passive girl.

Social behaviorists, in studying the way speech develops, find that even as infants boys and girls respond differently. The girl baby listens to her parents more intently, they claim, and therefore the parents pay more linguistic attention to girls. Boy babies tend to interrupt the parents' metacommunication and often get short shrift from the parents.

THE PROGRAMMED MESSAGE

Does the parent teach the child, or does the child teach the parent? Most likely it's a little of both. Parents too have metasignals programmed into them. "I know my baby," Mother insists. "One cry and I can tell what he wants." But what does Mother know? Not the words, for there are none yet, but the metasignal, and part of that knowing is instinctive.

The baby cries and Mother, halfway through her own meal, starts up from the table. "He's hungry. I'll put the bottle on now."

Father, who hasn't been programmed genetically or culturally to answer the crying, protests. "Let him cry a bit. Finish your meal. We don't have to jump up and run every time he lets out a peep."

The mother settles back, trying to ignore the cries, but finally she puts down her fork. "I can't eat while he's crying. I'll just be a second."

The discomfort Mother feels is a genetic turn-on, just as the cheeping of a baby bird turns on the feeding instinct in the mother bird. It is difficult, sometimes impossible, to resist this metasignal. Indeed, the signal is nature's device to insure the survival of the species.

This genetic metacommunication exists in animals and it is often without reason, a blind force. Have you ever seen a mother turkey when a predatory weasel comes into her pen? She rushes at him heroically and pecks furiously until he slinks away and her chicks are safe. Is it dedicated mother love in the human sense? Not at all. It is genetically programmed animal metacommunication.

An animal behaviorist, Dr. W. Schleidt, set out to prove this. In the journal *Behaviour,* he reported that he had wired a weasel for sound so that it emitted the cheeping of a turkey chick, and then he turned it loose in a turkey's pen. The mother turkey calmly allowed the cheeping weasel to come in among her chicks and carry one off.

The next step in the experiment was to deafen the mother turkey surgically. The deafened mother then proceeded to peck her own chicks to death!

The mother turkey, the animal behaviorist decided, had been genetically programmed to attack any small animal that might harm her chicks. Since her chicks were the size of the weasel, she was also programmed so that a cheeping sound turned off her aggression. The weasel, carrying a transmitter that cheeped, was tolerated. Her own chicks, when she could not hear their cheeping, were treated aggressively.

As a built-in metacommunication signal, the cheeping worked, but the system did not respond to reason. The built-in signal in the human mother—a vague anxiety when her baby cries—does respond to reason. She wants to relieve the anxiety by feeding the baby, but if her pediatrician suggests that she ignore the crying to get the baby on a schedule, she can do it. It may be uncomfortable, but her reason triumphs over her genes. The baby eventually gets the metasignal of no response and shifts his own internal schedule.

From roughly fourteen weeks to six months, the growing baby plays with sound. He sings, laughs, explores his range, and makes noise for the sheer pleasure of it—an important step toward handling speech. He repeats *lalala* and *mamama* and *dadada* and then, as his vocal cords and tongue develop, he starts the leap forward to articulation. First come the lip sounds, *pp bb mm,* then the tongue sounds, *tt dd ll nn,* and then the back of the tongue, *kk gg.* He practices pure metacommunication, the complicated sounds that go with every emotion, and he begins to identify emotions and moods in other people's sounds.

This is the age when a baby is conditioned by metacommunication. For example, he will make a sound or hear a sound when he's happy, and that sound becomes associated with happiness as others are associated with anger, fear, or love.

But the association varies from culture to culture. One child in a soft-spoken family associates softness with normal speech. Voices are raised only in anger. In another family, the voice level is higher. They yell continually, and raised voices are associated with love and warmth. We must always look to the culture when we interpret metacommunication.

By the time the child fully enters family life, usually at a year and a half, he has become very skillful at picking up metasignals. No matter what his parents say, he understands what they really mean. He becomes aware of the contradictions between words and meaning. What psychiatrists call the double-bind message is a classic example. Take Shawn, only three years old, but a child who's been receiving double-bind messages all of his short life.

Shawn's parents are careful not to fight in front of him; in fact, they rarely raise their voices to each other. Yet Shawn knows that something is wrong, that Mom and Dad are always angry.

"Don't be mad!" he pleads defensively when he spills his milk.

"Mom's not mad, honey. Daddy put it too near the edge." Turning to her husband, she says, "Hand me the sponge, dear, so I can clean it up."

It seems a simple, even a loving request. The word *dear* is thrown in, but Shawn hears nothing simple or loving in the tone. He hears the tight anger in his mother's voice, the sarcasm behind the *dear* and the unfair emphasis on the *I*.

On the surface his parents are sending a word message that everything is fine in this normal family, but the metasignals behind the words say everything is not fine. Shawn cannot deal with these continual contradictions, and he reacts by constantly apologizing in an attempt to relieve his own anxiety and assuage his parents' hidden anger.

By the time Shawn is ready to step into the outside world of nursery and school, he is thoroughly familiar with his parents' metasignals. He may not be happy with them, but he knows them. In the unfamiliar world outside, however, he may be thrown for a loss again. He'll have to take another few years to adjust to people who mean what they say, and he'll always carry with him that early double-bind message, *Don't believe what the words mean.*

Even happy children have to learn new types of metacommunication outside the home, and this is the time of life when speech defects often start, disturbances in rhythm, stammering and stuttering, a return to baby talk or unusual silences. But in most cases, as the child grows into the culture, he learns to cope with the people he meets outside his home.

METAMODELS

All children, during this period, look for older people they can copy and imitate. The boy becomes masculinized by his father, his brothers, his friends, and the television and movie heroes he sees. He learns to copy their metacommunication while his sister is copying her mother, her big sister, her friends, and her own TV and movie heroines.

TV heroes, detectives, cowboys, double agents may be presented as lacking in emotion; the growing boy will then adapt "cool" into his metavocabulary. The growing girl may copy the beautiful diction, the lisp or the sexual tones of a TV actress even as she copies her hair style.

These media metamodels have a powerful effect on the growing child. A recent experiment in a New York City school presented a class of poor black children with unusual black metamodels, lawyers, doctors, and writers. For the first time the children saw people of their own race in desirable, privileged, and intellectual roles.

For a while, one of the observers noted, the children

couldn't identify with them. The idea of blacks who were successful in these "establishment" areas seemed too strange. It was only when the guests began to talk to the children that metacommunication took over. The children recognized and trusted the undercurrents in the guests' voices. They suddenly became aware that these were their own people. They could communicate with them.

The soft burr of the black speech had not been completely erased, and though everything about the guests, from their clothes to their professions, spelled white, the metasignals in their voices spelled black. The children relaxed, began to ask questions, and came out of the sessions with completely different self-appraisals.

In this case, the guests, black professionals, had made their mark in the white world. They understood and used the metacommunication of that world, but they had not lost the metacommunication of their original culture.

In America, no matter what our economic class, we all have an overlay of accent, Northern or Southern, rural or urban, East Coast, West Coast, or Middle America. Sometimes the accent has a positive effect on communication, as it did with the class of city black children, but sometimes the effect can be disastrous. Take the case of Charlie Thompson, an enterprising real-estate agent in Fairmont, a small town in Ohio.

The Fairmont Ridge Subdivision had just sold its first three-acre parcel to Ralph Jones, a young lawyer from Chicago, and Charlie had introduced Ralph to his own builder for some estimates on a house.

"It was the damndest thing," Charlie told his wife that night. "We met up on the ridge where Ralph wanted the house, just the three of us, Al Bufford, my contractor, Ralph Jones, and me, and right from the start everything went wrong."

"But why, Charlie?" his wife asked. "Al's work is good and his prices are the best around."

"I know that and Ralph knows it too because I just showed him a house Al built, and he agreed it was a fantastic deal—but that was before he met him. This morning, when we all got together, it just hit the fan. Nothing Al said was right as far as Ralph was concerned. The deal was off the minute Al opened his mouth."

"I don't understand it."

"And I don't either. Hell, I know Al's good, but even before I saw his work I liked him. There's something about the guy that makes you want to trust him, but Ralph challenged everything he said, and you know, afterward he was annoyed with me because I introduced them. What the hell went wrong?"

Charlie never found out. Eventually Ralph Jones selected another builder, and even though his final estimate was higher he stuck with him. The good relationship that Charlie and Ralph had started with was spoiled that day, and when Ralph's brother-in-law came to town looking for a house, he went to a different agent. Charlie never understood what had happened, nor did Al Bufford.

And yet what spoiled the deal was a simple matter of metacommunication. If we look at Ralph Jones, Charles Thompson, and Al Bufford objectively, we see three men: a lawyer, a real-estate agent, and a builder. They are all in their thirties, intelligent, honest, and potentially able to help one another. There's nothing bad about that. But a closer look at each man can give us some clues to what went wrong.

Ralph Jones had moved to Fairmont from Chicago, where he worked for a law firm devoted to civil-rights cases, giving a great deal of his own time to causes he believed in. The last one was that of a long-haired young man who had been arrested in a small Southern town on what he claimed was a trumped-up marijuana charge. It had boiled down to prejudice on both sides, the "hippie from the North" against those "rednecks from the South."

Charlie Thompson was from the South originally, but he had lived in Fairmont long enough to lose his Southern accent. He had a reputation as a good agent and that was why Ralph Jones had come to him.

Al Bufford was from the South too. He had come north recently to start his own building firm. He still had his heavy Southern accent and a good many Southern mannerisms.

The stage was set. When Charlie met Al he felt an instant sense of kinship and comfortable identification. Without being consciously aware of it, Al's accent put him at ease. Here was a man he was sure he could trust because of that very familiarity.

When Ralph Jones met Charlie Thompson, he found a pleasant-spoken man who came highly recommended. He offered a good deal and Ralph accepted it. But when he met Al Bufford, all the subtle metacommunication came into play. Ralph heard only the Southern accent that he associated with "prejudice" and "rednecks." He bristled and refused to hear beyond the accent. His distrust broadened to include Charlie Thompson too, and the whole deal went sour. Yet Ralph Jones was never consciously aware of what made him dislike Al Bufford. Al's accent said one thing to Charlie and something entirely different to Ralph—yet the accent remained the same.

In any conversation, the background of the listener, how he thinks, what he has encountered before, what he believes, who he knows, where he comes from, what he did plus a hundred other factors are important elements in how he interprets what he hears. No two of us hear the same thing even when we listen to the same words. In the same way, no two people say the same thing even when they speak exactly the same words. They add to their words their own unique metacommunication.

At the funeral of a close friend, two men tell the widow, "I loved John." Each says exactly the same thing, but the way they say it is so different that the widow knows that only one of them really loved her husband.

Jim returns from a miserable and frustrating day at the office and his wife asks, "Did you have a nice day?" Her metasignals are all caring, but he hears irony and perhaps sarcasm because of what he went through.

Bob, a carpenter, hits his finger with a hammer and says, "Oh Christ!" To one worker nearby it's a simple expression of pain. To another, deeply religious, it's a blasphemy.

FUN WITH DICK AND JANE

Dick walks into a singles bar and sees Jane, an attractive woman. He starts a conversation by saying, "Hey, this is a cool place." The metasignal he throws out is *I'd like to get to know you*.

Jane looks at him angrily and through clenched teeth snaps, "I hate this joint!"

Bewildered, Dick backs away. His metasignals should not have initiated such a reaction. What's gone wrong? He doesn't know that Jane has been in the bar for two uncomfortable hours and had a disturbing experience with a man who blatantly propositioned her. She suddenly saw the whole scene as demeaning and empty. She was just about to leave when Dick spoke to her. Without knowing what she had gone through, there was no way Dick could have said the right thing.

All of these incidents, the funeral, the carpenter, the husband who came home from a rough day, Dick and Jane's encounter in the bar, occurred because of the subjective factor in any communication. It is one of the most difficult factors to deal with. How can we ever be aware of all that has happened to the person we are talking to? If we know them well, we can get hints from all the body-language signals they send out, but every human being has a secret subjective life that colors everything he hears or says.

These are the things over which we have no control, but we can control the metasignals we send out ourselves if we are conscious of what is going on. In the singles bar, Dick could have changed the subject at once when he sensed the anger in Jane's voice.

Any exchange between two people is complicated by a number of identities. For example, with Dick and Jane, there is the *Real Dick* and the *Real Jane*, but there is also the *Dick Jane Sees* and the *Jane Dick Sees*. This will depend on the image they each project. Is Jane wearing jeans and a T-shirt? That's one feminine image. Is she wearing a long skirt and a ruffled blouse? Another image. Is her hair long, short, bleached, or what? And what about Dick? Is he wearing an open shirt, gold chains around his neck? Or a business suit and a tie? These are props to project an image-of-the-week, an image that may be nothing like the real Dick.

There is also the *Dick Dick Would Like to Be*. This may be nothing like the *Real Dick*, or the image he tries to project. There is the *Jane Jane Would Like to Be*, and also the *Dick Jane Wants to See* and the *Jane*

Dick Wants to See—a total of eight people interacting instead of the two we met.

Does it all matter? Very much. Until they get to know each other very well—and sometimes not even then—Dick will never address the *Real Jane*, nor Jane the *Real Dick*. They'll speak to the Dick and Jane they see, and they'll hear as the Dick and Jane they'd like to be.

It gets very confusing, but fortunately there are techniques for cutting through the different façades. Metacommunication is one. For the most part we use metasignals automatically, unaware that we do so, and that very unawareness can break through to the real person. Dick may fancy himself as a James Bond type, but some metasignal in his voice will tell Jane that he is really a caring, emotional person. She may flatter him by accepting his Mr. Cool persona, but she responds to the real Dick underneath. Metacommunication has tipped her off.

In turn, Jane may think of herself as tremendously sophisticated, but her metaclues tell Dick that under the sophistication is a very vulnerable woman. He responds to that vulnerability while he plays along with the fantasy of sophisticated Jane.

Being sensitive to other people's vulnerabilities and strengths is the first step toward dealing with them. It's the beginning of true communication.

Each of us has as many different faces as Dick and Jane, and once we become aware of them and aware that metacommunication is influenced by them we are on our way to understanding the kind of person we are, what we would like to be, and how others see us.

2

Signal Variations

WHAT MAKES SPEECH

There are at least eleven accepted theories of how humans originally developed language. One even ties up speech with the way we use our hands. But whatever theory we accept, the ability to speak is still somewhat of a mystery. Man speaks because he wishes to be heard; he listens because he wishes to learn.

The way we put our thoughts into words and our words into sentences may be the result of a unique combination of the physical and the mental—the shape of our mouths and tongues, the structure of our vocal cords combined with the convolutions of our brains.

Sound, the basic element of speech, starts with breathing. The sounds develop as we push our breath past our vocal cords, those two small bands of tissue in our larynx. It is the shape of these cords, their length and thickness, as well as their tension that determines the pitch of our voices. When we talk, we can vary our pitch by changing the shape and tension of our cords. This happens without our being aware of it.

Try placing your fingers on either side of your vocal cords, just below your Adam's apple, and run your voice up and down the scale. You can feel the cords change shape as they vibrate.

We make our voices louder by pushing our breath past our vocal cords faster and more forcefully. But to avoid too much strain on our lungs and our cords, nature has designed us somewhat like a musical instrument. A violin, for example, produces sound when its strings vibrate. Then the sound is resonated and mellowed by the hollow body of the instrument. Our voices, in a similar way, are resonated and reinforced by hollow cavities in our bodies. The space behind the nostrils and above the roof of the mouth is one of these cavities. The mouth itself is another. The throat is a third, and the larynx and trachea leading down to the chest is the fourth. When they resonate, the entire chest joins in.

None of these resonators is as rigid as a violin. Our tissues are flexible, and our muscles can change the size and rigidity of all our body cavities—and change the quality of the sound that they resonate.

For the most part the intricate phonation of speech takes place in the mouth, but some sounds, *m, n,* and *ng,* are routed through the nose. Try holding your nostrils and pronouncing any of them. You can hear the unpleasant nasal sound. This is what is called an adenoidal voice. It may signal one thing to the person who uses it, but something else, something very irritating, to the person who hears it.

Of course, this is true of every aspect of communication, and especially true of metacommunication. What you intend as a pleasant remark may be heard as a sarcastic one; what you intend as irony may be taken literally. Different resonances and registers mean different things to different people. The whine in a child's voice may be saying, "I'm tired and frightened. Comfort me!" But the parent may interpret the whine as "I'm going to wear your resistance down!"

THE BREATH OF SPEECH

We breathe to speak, but even more important, we breathe to live, and what affects our lives affects our breath. Fat people and thin people breathe differently and speak differently, and so do active and passive people and healthy and sick ones. Heavy smoking, hay fever and heart disease, asthma, allergies, emphysema, and a host of other troubles all have an effect on breathing—and on speaking.

Some psychologists have speculated on a link between breathing and personality. They suggest that the deep breather is a go-getter, while his shallow-breathing friend tends to be a intellectual, a dreamer. This may be true, but perhaps the go-getter needs to breathe deeply in order to pull in enough oxygen to go-out-and-get. It's true that we need less oxygen when we daydream, but some intellectuals are go-getters, some college professors are long-distance runners, and many shallow breathers are neither intellectuals nor dreamers.

Any link between breathing and personality seems tenuous at best, but there is a link between breathing and our emotions. When we're overcome by grief or frustration, when we're fatigued, hopeless, or depressed, we breathe shallowly. When we're excited, angry, or keyed up we breathe deeply. Since emotions are reflected in metacommunication, there is a very strong connection between breathing and the metasignals we send out.

Take a look at Carl, an advertising executive, and hear the way he reacts to an emotional situation. He calls his wife on the phone and gasps out, "It's happened! It all hit the fan today."

"What happened?" His wife is frightened. Carl is breathing so rapidly he can hardly get his words out. His breathing signals either fear or excitement. "Oh God, are you all right?" The rush of anxiety in her voice slows Carl up a bit.

"I'm all right, but it's fantastic!"

She realizes that the fright message is wrong, and she zeros in on the excitement. Breathing more slowly herself, she says, "Slow down, honey. Take a couple of deep breaths, and then tell me all about it."

Carl puts down the receiver and does just that, then, a few seconds later, breathing normally, he explains that there's been a big shake-up at the agency. Heads rolled, but fortunately he's come out on top.

The rapid breathing of Carl's excitement colored his words, but at first his wife couldn't be sure just what the color was, *fear* or *extreme joy*

Most of us have moments when we signal contradictory emotions with the same metasignal. Extreme joy, fear, irritability, excitement, anxiety—all are sent out by rapid breathing. The listener must search for other clues in the voice to separate one emotion from another. For Carl's wife, the clue was, "I'm all right." Then she could relax.

In the same contradictory way, shallow breathing can signal either fatigue or thoughtfulness, hopelessness or meditation, grief and frustration, or calm and gentleness. The listener must always be alert to other metaclues, resonance, speed, pitch, volume, or any of the other multitude of elements that carry our words, as well as the words themselves.

Breathing, whether it's rapid or slow, deep or shallow, affects the pattern of the voice, and it also affects the speed of speech and vocal punctuation. How we pause between each word in a sentence and the length of these pauses send signals to the listener about the importance of what we're saying. The longer the pause, the deeper the feeling we communicate. But if the pause is too long, the depth of feeling registers as pomposity or even exaggeration.

Short pauses between words signal that we're *together, organized, definite*. But if the pause is too short, the listener may get an impression of coldness, even furtiveness.

Along with the pauses between the words, there is the speed at which the words are spoken. We speak quickly when we're eager to get our message out. The words may rush forth, stumbling and tumbling over each other, and our listener hears an immediacy in our voice. The fast talker can be both persuasive and expressive, but if he comes on too fast, he risks irritating or boring his listener.

Don is a fast talker. His friends say he makes them nervous because he's too keyed up. Don fires his words as if they were machine-gun bullets triggering off his barrage of ideas. He makes his listeners uncomfortable, and they, in turn, see him as spastic. Part of Don's speech pattern is the unconscious fear that someone will interrupt him before he is finished. He seems to be on the offensive, but his verbal barrage is really a defense against his own uncertainty. Whatever metasignal Don is trying to send out, most of his listeners react with irritation.

Some people who talk at a normal speed may quicken their tempo when what they have to say is awkward or embarrassing. Father asks his daughter, "Why are you so late bringing the car back?"

His daughter's words rush out with furious speed. "I couldn't help it, like I had to drop Carol off and you wouldn't believe it, but Annie lost a contact lens, and then we had to . . ."

She is on shaky ground. If she talks fast enough, perhaps the words themselves will pave the way to a safer spot. Her brother is a fast talker too when he wants to be. He listens to his sister's explanation and interjects a quick "What a load of bullshit!" but so quickly that his father barely catches it.

Like Brother, most of us talk swiftly when what we have to say is socially unacceptable. Some storytellers may be able to drag out a dirty joke, but most tellers rush through the story, or at least the punch line, blurring the awkward words together.

While the fast talker is eager to get it all out, the slow talker is usually reluctant. His metasignal may be negative, a message of indifference, and his lazy pace will turn his listener off. But on the positive side, another slow talker can signal conviction, thoughtfulness, interest, and sincerity.

Put a fast and a slow talker together and watch the misunderstanding grow. Each is bewildered by the metasignals of the other. If the slow speaker does get a chance to talk, the fast speaker often ends up impatiently finishing every sentence for him. Long pauses, drawn-out words make the fast speaker uneasy, while rapid, run-together sentences leave the slow talker speechless. There is often a communication breakdown.

"He's an arrogant windbag," Slow Talker thinks.

Fast Talker, in turn, wonders why Slow Talker is so cold and withdrawn.

THE BEAT AND RHYTHM

Apart from the speed of speech and the quality that breath lends to it there is a beat and a rhythm that varies from person to person and from language to language. Every song has its rhythm, and so does every old-fashioned poem. But there is also a rhythm in normal speech. We say, "How are you?" with an emphasis on *are*. If we were to emphasize *how*, the rhythm would be thrown off, and so would the meaning. *How* are you? doesn't make sense.

Before a baby can talk, he imitates the rhythm of adult speech. In doing so, he is sending out pure metasignals. In a limited way, this lets him communicate some of his emotions and feelings to his parents. Later, he will add words to the rhythmic sounds. Eventually he acquires sentences and then the language. Each step up the linguistic ladder is helped by the new words, concepts, and metasignals he picks up and tries out.

Most of us are not concerned with the rhythm of our speech. We have absorbed it from the people we hear, and we've learned that within certain limits it can be altered. Often, talking to young children, we adopt a singsong rhythm to comfort or calm them. The words are unimportant, but the metamessage says, "I will take care of you."

The same metasignal used by a mother talking to a grown son can be troubling instead of comforting—at least to the son's wife. Alison complains, "It really drives me up the wall when Norman's mother calls him baby, honey, sweetheart. She sounds as if she's talking to a two-year-old." Alison imitates not only her mother-in-law's words, but also the singsong rhythm in her voice. She is upset at the metacommunication that says her husband is still a little boy as far as Mama is concerned.

Listening to the rhythms of communication between two people who are emotionally close, you can often pick up clues to their relationship. Norman was always his mother's little boy, and Alison could hear it in her voice when she wanted him to do something for her.

In the public arena, a clever speaker can shift the normal rhythm of speech to hammer home certain points. Hitler was so well aware of this that he often had his speeches accompanied by drum rolls to key his listeners' pulses to the rousing rhythm of his speech. Their own racing pulse gave listeners an additional metamessage of excitement added to his words.

Some politicians have a comfortable rhythmic flow, and we hear it as part of their total charisma. The smoothness of John Kennedy was, in part, a smoothness of rhythm when he spoke. Jimmy Carter's speaking lacks that smoothness. His pauses are awkward and often he omits the rhythmic clues that tell us whether he has or hasn't finished a sentence.

The metamessage this awkwardness signals may not be all bad. For some, his hesitation signals earnestness and he comes across as sincere. However, for others it signals uncertainty and a lack of strength.

Impersonators depend heavily on the peculiarities of speech rhythm. A good female impersonator seldom uses a falsetto. Instead he adopts a female beat or rhythm, and adds to it the unique rhythm of the person he is imitating.

PITCH, RESONANCE, AND REGISTER

We compared the speaking human to a musical instrument, and the resemblance starts with the vocal cords. We tighten the strings on a violin to raise its pitch, and we tighten our vocal cords to raise the pitch of our voices. If we feel something deeply—anger, fear, joy—our bodies, including our vocal cords, tense up.

Conversely, when we're depressed or overly tired, our muscles sag and our vocal cords lose their tension. We speak in a low-pitched voice. Traditionally, the depressed voice is soft, dull, and monotonous. The agitated voice, on the other hand, is high-pitched and tight—and often out of control.

In normal speech our pitch varies, but not as high or low as it does in fear and depression. Pitch gives variety to our tones; resonance gives them body. If we are born with heavy vocal cords of the right shape and a good chest, we can produce deep, mellow, earthy tones. We can speak comfortably in a chest register. If our cords are shaped differently, thinner and tighter, we can resonate through the head and speak in high, thin, heavenly tones.

Singers must control their resonance. Joe Turner, Marian Anderson, Joe Williams all resonate their voices through their chests, while Beverly Sills, Barbra Streisand, Mildred Bailey are sopranos and resonate through their heads. Someone like Sarah Vaughan can use the high or the low register successfully.

But singers are not the only ones who control the resonance of their voices. We all manage it, though many of us are unaware of what we are doing. We use the different resonances to convey different metamessages. We speak in deep chest tones to signal strength, dependability, firmness, solidity. The Victorian father resonated from the chest to come up with an authoritarian voice. The father of today tries raising his voice to produce the same metamessage, but just increasing the volume doesn't do it. Instead it signals spontaneity and lack of control. Resonance signals something more deliberate. The watchful child can read both messages and figure out which father means business.

Father may use deep tones to signal strength and dependability, but a low resonance isn't confined to him alone. When Mother speaks in a low register we know that she means what she's saying.

A woman with a low voice, low in register and pitch, sounds self-assured and we're inclined to trust her. Some women use the low register to come on sexually. Julie London, the singer, does a commercial for television in a low, husky register, and it literally oozes sex. Her normal register is much higher, but with practice and control she has learned how to send the low metasignals.

Because a low register signals strength in men and women, it doesn't always follow that someone who speaks in a high register is not strong and determined. Many people have inappropriate voices for their personalities. When they talk their metasignals get in the way and sometimes contradict what they are saying. It's as if the message were wrapped and delivered in the wrong package.

Lila, a head buyer in a large Chicago department store, is a victim of metamismatch. She is responsible, talented, and determined, but she speaks in a tiny, high-pitched voice that throws many of the salesmen off. They hear what she is saying, but behind the words they read the metasignal *I am vulnerable and uncertain*.

They react to it by coming on as big, strong men. Seeing Lila as a helpless woman, they try to snow her with merchandise she doesn't need. They're bewildered at first, and then annoyed, when they discover that she is more than their equal in business.

Lila is unaware of how her voice affects others. She doesn't know that she has copied the little-girl voice from her mother and aunts. She complains that most of the men in her business are operators or male chauvinists. She can hold her own, but a lot of the friction and misunderstanding would be lessened if she could tune in on her own conflicting metasignals.

The paradox of resonance and register is not confined to women. "I liked Abner the minute I met him. It was his voice," Amy said. "He's a real man." But she's judging him not on what he says or does, but on the resonant middle register of his voice. Bill, Abner's friend, speaks with a higher resonance, using his nasal cavities to resonate his voice. His voice is high and thin. Recently he was being considered for a top job in his firm. The competition was tough, and when it narrowed down to Bill and another guy, it was the chairperson of the board who had the final say. He voted against Bill. Why?

Walking out of the meeting, he told a colleague, "They're both good men, but I don't think Bill is right for the job. He's a good worker and a nice guy, but I get an uneasy feeling when I listen to him. He sounds indecisive. Not enough strength."

Yet Bill, like Lila is a strong, capable person. Unfortunately, like Lila, he is also sending out contradictory messages.

VOICE CHANGES

Can Lila and Bill change their contradictory metasignals? It isn't easy, but it can be done. The first step is to hear themselves as others do. A tape recorder with good fidelity will do the trick. It's best to let a little time go by between taping and listening. It makes for objectivity. The person who can really hear himself as others do and then determines to change his voice must decide if it's too high or too low. Is his pitch right? What about his register? Shall he change that too?

But of all the questions he asks about his own voice, the most important is, "Does my voice refect what I want to say?" "Are my metasignals in tune with my words?" "Is there anything about the way I use my voice, the way I form the words, that turns people off?"

Once you have picked up what might be wrong, you can decide how you want your voice to change. You can, by practice, widen your pitch range or shift your resonance. You can slow your speech or speed it up.

Start by reading or speaking into a tape recorder, then play it back. Experiment with your voice. Lower it, raise it, try out all your resonating places, and always keep in mind just how you would like to sound.

One friend whose pitch was so low that she had trouble making herself heard practiced by acting out all the parts in *Who's Afraid of Virginia Woolf?*. As she said later, "I went through every emotion from A to Z, and I made my voice work for me. Not that I'm like the characters in the play, but after listening to myself on the recorder I realized that I tend to speak in a very flat voice. It may be because I come from a family where too open a display of emotion was considered vulgar. My mom used to say, 'Only lower-class people show their emotions when they talk.' I guess a lot of that rubbed off on me."

This young woman was right. Her own voice communicated a complete lack of emotion every time she opened her mouth. Her low, flat voice said, "I couldn't care less about the things I'm saying." She lacked a basic quality of good speech, *melody*.

THE MELODY LINGERS ON

What is melody? We never really understood it until we met Irv. He was someone who had mastered melody to the point where it became a source of great amusement for his friends. Irv could always be counted on to liven up a draggy evening with his Russian "shtick." He could do Gromyko addressing the United Nations, a dissident renouncing the Soviet Union, a ballet dancer defecting to the West—and his mimicry was so perfect that once a visiting Russian friend listened to him in absolute bewilderment.

"He's talking nonsense, you know, but I'm confused. It sounds so much like Russian!"

And it did. Part of it was Irv's facial expressions, but more important was the *melody* he gave to the gibberish he spoke. He used Russian phonemes and roots to make up his gibberish, but he inflected them as Russian is inflected, and even though there was no real language in his talk, his metacommunication was perfect, his melody was exact.

There is a melody to speech, and it includes all the metasignals we use. It is a complex combination of pitch and register and resonance, speed and rhythm and volume range. Every language, every dialect of a language, sings its own melody. Melody is affected by grammatical structure, emotional value, moods and attitudes, and the melody of a conversation can signal love or hate or indifference—even when no more than one word is spoken.

A husband comes home from work, and at the dinner table he asks his wife, "Hey, do you know what happened at work today?"

The wife says, "No," and with that single syllable establishes a relationship, not by the word but by the melody behind it. If the no is flat, without melody, she signals lack of interest: *I couldn't care less about what you did. I have my own problems.*

If she drawls her no out into almost three syllables, rising on the second, her melody says, *Tell me. I'm interested.* It also says, *I care. I'm concerned.*

A rising melody like this one signals excitement; a declining melody signals despair. Try it on some simple sentences. Are you going out? Did you have a good time? Even the one we all want to hear, I love you. Drop your voice on the you and there is no conviction behind it.

Lose the melody, the music in your voice, and you lose most of your metacommunication. You say nothing beyond the words, and your meaning is empty. The cold, unfeeling voice that transmits nothing, that shares nothing, that never moves out of itself, is the voice without melody, without song.

3

The Loud and the Soft of It

THE VOLUME WEAPON

Teaching apes to communicate has become a full-time project at a number of universities and animal-behavior centers across the country. If apes are taught the symbols of communication, the reasoning goes, if they are taught a language, then they may learn to think in that language, and we may learn to do what Dr. Dolittle did—talk to the animals.

Animals, of course, have been communicating with each other successfully since the first self-replicating cell searched for a similar cell in the pre-Cambrian ooze. Without a language, animals have had to depend on body movement; once they developed lungs, they added grunts and groans and barks and moans. After animals developed vocal cords, roars and purrs and all the variations in between became more popular. Very early on, volume, that most useful metasignal, was perfected.

Volume can be a very successful vocal weapon. Noise frightens the enemy. The male gorilla, a gentle animal, beats his chest and roars when a stranger invades his territory. Proto-man probably did the same thing, and every modern man knows that a loud, angry voice is an effective weapon in any argument—though with civilization he has also learned how deadly soft anger can be, how destructive a whispered word often is.

In prehistoric days, when one ragged horde of men stormed the stronghold of another tribe, some healthy bass probably led them with a loud, "Yell, you guys! Yell like hell!"

It's not such a far jump from our club-swinging, bellowing ancestors to a group of pom-pom-waving cheerleaders screaming, "Let's hear it for the home team! Yell like hell! 'Ray team!"

In group yelling there is strength, and as a friend once confided, yelling can also work when you're backed against the wall. "I was only nine years old when I discovered the power of a loud voice," he explained. "Our gang had built a hut on this empty lot and one day another bunch of kids sneaked over to demolish it. We were pretty scared. Me, I was a skinny little runt, but I had a deep voice and I started using it, yelling, 'God damn you, get the hell out of here!'

"They hesitated and I shouted even louder, and then they turned and ran! I was a hero, just because I yelled as loud as I could."

A soft answer may "turneth away wrath," but there are times when a loud one works pretty well too. Consider the scene in a large meeting room where a working session in salesmanship has been going on for six hours, nonstop. Thirty men in shirt sleeves are sitting at tables, a bit wild-eyed, tired, their ties loosened and all of them fed up to the neck with slogans and suggestions.

Now the leader looks around and suddenly jumps up. "Are you going to make that sale? Tell me!" he demands loudly.

There are a few head nods and a few tired Yesses. "No!" he shouts. "I want to hear you say it. *I'll make that sale!*"

The Yesses are stronger.

He turns his own volume up, his voice booming out over the room. "Louder. Shout it out. *I'll make that sale!*"

"I'll make that sale!" The response is sudden, electric. *"I'll make that sale!"*

As the speaker's voice urges them on, they respond by imitating not only his words and expression but also the tremendous volume of his voice. The room rocks with their revitalized enthusiasm. Their tiredness evaporates and they begin to feel confident, powerful.

Afterward the men leave, excited, keyed up, and ready to go. *What a session! I feel great. Dynamite!*

What happened was the impact and power of positive volume. Shared yelling beefed up not only their enthusiasm but also their self-assurance. By shouting, the leader stimulated the group.

At an earlier session, he used a different trick to manipulate his audience. "The potential buyer is wavering." He lowered his voice dramatically. "That's when you go in for the kill." The group, in turn, responded to his theatrical whisper with murmurs of "Right. Move in. Make the sale!"

The leader had learned to use his voice like an instrument, to go up and down the volume scale when it was called for. A loud voice signaled enthusiasm and confidence; a soft one said, *Trust me. I have something special for you.*

All of us know how to regulate the sound on our TVs or stereos. When it's too loud or too soft we deliberately change it. However, we are not so deliberate about changing our voice volume. We often become so involved in what we're saying that we forget to tune our volume properly. Yet we are bothered when someone else speaks too loudly or too softly because unlike the stereo or TV they cannot be tuned to a comfortable level.

A MATTER OF STATUS

There are rules for the use of volume in communication, just as there are rules for all the elements of language. For example, a person of high status may raise his voice to someone of lower status; a foreman may yell at a worker, a teacher at a student, a parent at a child, a husband at a wife—or a wife at a husband—depending on who rules the roost.

Men generally feel free to dominate a woman vocally, and in return, many women use a soft voice as a defense against this kind of domination. The metamessage of their low voice says, *Don't attack me, because I am helpless against the aggressive onslaught of your voice. I am lowering my own to show how defenseless I am.*

If, in an argument or discussion, a woman raises her voice, her metamessage changes to *Don't attack me, because I'm going to stand up for myself!*

You can lower your voice for effectiveness if you have enough self-assurance, or if you have the advantage of clout. A few years ago we were both associated with a top television executive, a man with tremendous clout. During important meetings he deliberately lowered his voice so that everyone had to lean forward to hear him. He always held center stage.

"If anyone under me doesn't hear what I say the first time," he used to boast, "he won't be around for a second try. I don't give a damn who it is, producer, writer, or some little typist. I want full attention when I speak."

In spite of his low voice, he wasn't a subtle man. Everyone who worked for him was aware of his manipulative games, but they were also aware of his status and power. Unlike this executive, few of us use a low voice for emphasis. We feel that authority goes with loudness, just as weakness and vulnerability go with softness. We tend to judge people on the basis of how loud or soft their voices are, and while sometimes we are right, we are more often wrong. In the same way we may be intimidated by a loud voice, and still use loudness against those who cannot defend themselves.

Listen to a mother shopping with her small children in a supermarket, to a teacher in a poor urban school, to a civil servant in a welfare office, or to an adult talking to his elderly parent. Inevitably the sound goes up as the voice becomes a weapon against the vulnerable.

A close friend, suffering from paralysis of the vocal cords, was recuperating on a cruise vacation. In a letter home, she wrote, "The perception you develop when you join the ill is amazing. One passenger, a pleasant enough young man, approached me and said, 'Look at the red sails on those boats.' I couldn't answer him, except for my usual croak, so I smiled and croaked a bit.

"He immediately raised his voice and repeated his statement. When I croaked again, his voice went up another decibel. The more I signaled my helplessness, the louder he shouted. He made me feel like an idiot!"

THE CULTURAL CONTRADICTION

The metacommunication of volume often causes problems when two different cultures come together. John and Karen, a young married couple, came from different backgrounds. In Karen's family, everyone spoke softly. A low voice was the norm. Her parents raised their voices only when they were angry or under stress. Karen's low voice gave the impression that she was shy, but she wasn't. She was quiet, and it was that very quietness that attracted John.

He came from a boisterous family. Everyone shouted. They shouted when they were happy, and they shouted when they were angry. Their normal range of conversation was several octaves above Karen's shouting voice—or so it seemed to her.

Once the honeymoon was over and the moonglow off, cultural contradictions set in. The night of John's family's first visit, Karen murmured, "Thank heavens!" as the last one left. "Now we can have a little peace and quiet."

Hurt and defensive, John said, "What's been eating you all evening?"

"The way you scream at each other. All that shouting."

"Shouting? Who was shouting? That's just the way we talk. At least we don't sit around like scared rabbits not opening our mouths."

"Is that the way you see me?" Karen's voice was tight and low, and they were off, into their first married quarrel. They patched it up later, but that night was just the beginning of a long, difficult ordeal for both, each misreading the metacommunication of the other's family. Karen interpreted the loudness in John's family as insensitivity. She found them overbearing, while John knew they were warm and caring people.

On the other hand, Karen's parents' and brother's low voices put him off. He felt that they didn't like him, that they were withdrawn, cold, and unfriendly.

What neither could understand was that one person's loud or soft is another person's normal. In interpreting metacommunication, we must take into account not only our own background but the other person's as well. How could John and Karen have handled their problem without hurting the people involved? The first step must be awareness. John could try explaining to someone in his family that their boisterous, loud voices upset his wife. Let's try a sample dialogue.

"Look, Ma, it's not that Karen's shy. She just isn't used to the way we holler at each other."

"Who hollers?" John's mother asks, bewildered.

"We do. At least it seems that way to Karen. We've got to give her a chance to talk."

"In my house everyone talks!"

"Ma!" John yells. "Listen to me!"

"I'm listening!" his mother's voice booms back, and then the two of them begin to laugh, both realizing how loud they are. The awareness is there, and with it an accommodation to Karen's problem is possible. Later, when the two come to dinner, John's mother becomes Karen's champion. "Hold it down. We're all yelling. Let Karen say a word."

If Karen can understand that John has the same problem in reverse in her family, that their low voices make him uncomfortable, then she can single someone out, perhaps her brother, to be the negotiator with her parents.

Most of us speak within a comfortable range of volume which varies with the situation and with the person we're talking to. Sometimes it's important to speak softly, even to whisper. Sometimes a loud, penetrating voice is needed to signal alarm, emphasis, or even joy. It is only when we discover that the volume of our everyday speech is annoying to others that we must learn to tune our voices up or down.

We can manage many situations by proper tuning. In a loud argument between two people, one can lower his voice, and by doing so force the other down a decibel or two. Often some anger and hostility will be dissipated along with the excess volume.

In panic or pain, a soft voice can reassure or comfort. It says, *I am here. I understand.* And most important, *I care.*

Conscious regulation of our volume can help us reinforce the positive qualities of our personality, or change the negative ones. The shy person who uses a diffident voice can bolster his self-confidence by raising his volume. He should try it gradually, starting with nonthreatening situations, asking a bus driver for directions, a store clerk for the price of an article, a friend for the loan of a book or tool.

On the other hand, someone who is aware that his loud voice is a part of a too aggressive nature could try lowering his volume to allow some of the more gentle aspects of his nature to surface. It all boils down to awareness first, and control second.

THE SOUNDS OF SILENCE

Whispering is an effective metasignal, and at one time or another we all use it.

"It's all right, sweetheart," the mother's soft whisper comforts her frightened child.

Under her breath, another woman whispers harshly to her rejecting lover, "I hate you."

And in still another situation, a husband uses a gentle whisper when he tells his wife that he loves her and she whispers back, "I love you too."

In all three cases, the whisper accentuates the intensity of the communication. A whispering voice can be intimate and caring, or rejecting and cruel. No matter what the whisper is saying, the metamessage says, *What I have to say is for your ears alone. No one else is involved in this conversation.*

There are times, of course, when we do not whisper to exclude others. We see a lovely sunset, hear a moving piece of music, listen to a poem, and our voice drops. We whisper, "How lovely." It is as if we might destroy the fragile beauty of the moment by raising our voices; a whisper preserves the mood, keeps it intact.

Often we will drop our voice to a whisper when we are confronted with a fearful, unpleasant, or unhappy situation. How many of us seem to whisper instinctively in the presence of death or tragedy! The very word death causes some people to lower their voices. We whisper when we comfort the bereaved. Our murmured words become a comfort and a reassurance, not only to the other but to ourselves as well. Perhaps at times like this we seek to re-create the soothing whispers we remember from childhood, the caring, comforting sounds that Mother used when we were afraid.

Metacommunication teaches us to consider speech from a different angle and listen in a different way. We know that communication is not only the spoken word but also all the words we leave unsaid. Silence often carries an emotional impact that hits louder than words.

Silence is golden, but not when it is used as a weapon or a defense. A young man tells us, "My father was a cold man. He rarely spoke. There were these long silences while all of us waited for a word, an acknowledgment, anything to let us know he cared. It seemed to me then that he had no feelings, no love."

Another person sees her sister's silence as disapproval. "I don't visit Vivian anymore. I would start talking to her, telling her about the kids, and she'd clam up, sit there silently. I knew that she disapproved of me, of how I live and how I raise the children."

"My mother goes away from me," a teenager tries to explain. "She's not gone physically, but she might as well be. I don't even think she hears me . . . she sure doesn't answer me."

And yet, without silence, the world would be an intolerable place. We all need some degree of quietness, and being silent ourselves is sometimes the only way we can tell others that we would like a little privacy, a silent place in time, a space of our own.

In communication, there is a difference between the silence that is productive, that allows you to think, digest, and really listen to another person, and the silence that can say you're withdrawn, cold, distrustful, and uninvolved.

If you are a naturally quiet person, not a talker, start noticing how others react to your silence. Are they friendly toward you? Do they feel free to talk and be open with you? Do they seek you out to exchange ideas, thoughts, experiences, or even just to talk?

If they don't, analyze your own quietness. Perhaps you are too silent and you give the impression of uncaring coldness. You might ask yourself, "Am I silent because I'm afraid to speak, or because I feel embarrassed when I speak?" Or is it that you just don't want to be involved with others?

If you think silence is a problem to you, then try to become aware of how long and how often you are silent in social gatherings. Become aware of other people's silences. What are they telling you? Are they comfortable silences, or are they the silences of withdrawal?

We have friends, a married couple with a weekend house in the country. The wife told us, one evening, that as they left the city to drive there, conversation usually dwindled down, and for a good part of the hour and a half ride both of them were quiet. "This is particularly true when we drive up in the early evening. It is so pleasant to enjoy the silence, the quietness."

"But aren't you uncomfortable or bored?"

"Oh no. It's a reassuring silence. We both need the time to unwind, to be alone with ourselves. If either of us wants to talk, that's fine too. The other will listen. We're free to talk, but we're also free to be quiet."

They went on to tell us that last week they had driven a friend up with them. "She chattered endlessly during the entire trip. We like her, and usually we enjoy talking with her, but on that ride we both missed our quiet time. The constant need to listen and reply became a serious block to any real communication."

While some of us, like this couple, see each other's silences as intimate, and are comfortable in this form of communication, most of us have trouble handling silence in a close relationship. A young man confides to his friends, the night before his wedding, that he's really worried. "This may sound crazy, but I can't figure out what we are going to talk about every day of the year. Once you're married, do you have to keep talking all the time?"

One of his friends says, "I guess you don't, but I don't know. I'm still single."

"Even now if we're sitting around and I don't say much, she always asks me, 'What are you thinking?' She doesn't like it if I'm quiet, and then I get embarrassed and start looking for something to say. I don't want her to feel I'm dull, but there are times when I don't feel like talking."

The worried young groom-to-be has equated silence with dullness. He's learned from his culture that an aggressive, smart man is a talker. We are a nation of talkers, and we equate talking with doing. His fiancée has absorbed this too. She's uneasy when he's quiet because she suspects it may be because of a fault of hers. She's been brought up with the idea that women are listeners, men are talkers, and periods of silence are not a quiet kind of communication but a threat to their communion.

In the same way, the mother of a teenage boy admits that she feels disturbed when her son is silent, as he so often is. "I get the feeling that something's wrong."

"Is he sullen, or unhappy?"

"No . . . in fact, when he does talk, he's a lot of fun. It's just that he gets these periods of silence when he's with the family, and it bothers us.

"I ask him, 'What are you thinking?' and he says, 'Nothing, Mom.' How can anyone think about nothing?"

What the mother fails to realize is that his "nothing" is a simple statement of his need for privacy. We all need privacy, and we all find it in different ways. The boy found his in silence. The mother's interpretation of his silence was based on her own reaction. To her, silence was an exclusion, a metamessage that said, *I don't want to be part of the family*. On a deeper level, it spelled out a lack of control. As long as she knew everything about him, as long as he talked to her, she believed she was in charge of the relationship. She failed to grasp the metamessage that he was sending. *I need privacy, an inner space of my own. I must have my own life, a time when I am by myself, even in the same house as the rest of my family!*

THE INNER METAMESSAGES

No silence is without thought, according to many philosophers. They speculate that man couldn't think creatively before he had a language to think in. Thinking is very much like talking to yourself. Sometimes we even do it subvocally, and sometimes we do it out loud. A young woman, Jane, is waiting for a call from her newest guy. She tries to read, but she can't concentrate The phone rings, and in a tense whisper she begins to talk to herself. "It has to be him. Please let it be him!"

As she listens, knowing her roommate has picked up the phone, the silent words tumble around inside her head. "He said he'd call. I think he likes me. I know he thinks I'm fun—we had fun together—the way we laughed on that last date!"

"Jane, it's for you," her roommate calls, and as she hurries to the phone, Jane breathes a sigh of relief and tells herself, "Oh great, wonderful!"

Jane's inner dialogue with herself had an overlay of metacommunication. Her first reaction when the telephone rang was, *It has to be him!* Her words were positive. Then she began to give herself reassuring metamessages, comforting words . . . *he likes me . . . he thinks I'm fun . . . we had fun . . . we laughed. . . .* The reassuring words carry a metamessage of laughter, fun, and hope. They reassure her, and when she hears the call is for her she sums it up with *great, wonderful!*

Metamessages to ourselves can either help or hinder us. "I hope I can do the job. I'm as good as the other applicants they interviewed," the applicant says to himself as he goes into the personnel office. But his metamessage to himself contradicts his assurance. He is telling himself one thing, but he hears the anxiety and doubt in his voice and it undoes the assurance.

"I don't care what the teacher says. I understand the formula," the student tells himself, but the bravado of *I don't care* contradicts the certainty of *I understand the formula*. He is setting up protective barriers to cope with a situation he is uneasy about. He *does* care what the teacher says and he *doesn't* understand the work.

All of us must learn to listen to our inner communications. We should be aware of just how those communications affect us. Ask yourself, do you use self-deception rather than face up to the truth? If you do, are you sending contradictory and confusing signals to your inner self? Do you tell yourself one thing and then betray it with different metasignals? No matter how encouraging the words, is your inner self depressed, anxious, frightened? Do you really *hear* your thoughts and pick up all the emotional intensity of them? Some thoughts are loud, others soft, gentle, even insidious.

Learn to listen to yourself, not only *what* you are saying but also *how* you are saying it. Listen for the words you use inside your head, especially the emotion-laden ones.

Your secret self-communication is bristling with metasignals, and as you become aware of them, you will also become aware of just how much they influence your thoughts and your actions.

4

Static on the Metaband (or, Clearing the Airwaves)

THE SALESMAN AND THE SOCIOLOGIST

The controversy about which came first, the chicken or the egg, is easier to solve than the linguistic puzzler, Which came first, language or jargon? It's possible that the builders of the tower of Babel couldn't complete it because of too many technical ways of describing structural problems, not because of too many languages.

Jargon has always been a problem in communication, and probably always will be. All of us use it, and every family has a jargon of its own. There is a prison jargon and a medical jargon, a lawyer's jargon, a salesman's jargon, and, to our infinite sorrow, a political jargon. Does anyone understand, exactly, what any politician means?

There is a jargon for each generation. What was *jazzy* yesterday is *far out* today. And now, cutting across all generations, there is the jargon of the citizen-band radio. A *Willy Weaver* is a drunken driver, *Smokey* is a trooper, while *Smokey in a brown bag with ears* is a trooper in an unmarked car with a CB radio. A *downed four-wheeler* is a stalled car. The speed limit of 55 miles per hour is *double nickles* while speeding tickets are *invitations*—and so it goes.

Exactly what is jargon? Webster defines it as an "obscure and often pretentious language marked by circumlocutions and long words." A newer and meatier definition suggests that it's a way to express a simple idea in as many complicated words as possible.

But these definitions are made by scholars who fear that jargon can infiltrate the language to the point where its basic purity is lost. In truth, however, there is little *basic purity* to any language. Language cannot be frozen in time, and often jargon is so colorful and exciting that it becomes permanently incorporated into a language. Then, a hundred years later, scholars fight against losing that same jargon to some new expression. Jargon is, among other things, a potent force in any language's natural evolution.

Sometimes jargon can strengthen communication, but there are times when it can cloud it. It can be a shorthand to help members of the same profession understand each other, but it can also confuse someone outside the profession. Sidney and Rosa were victims of that inside-outside confusion.

They met at a friend's house and felt a sudden, electric attraction that promised a "meaningful relationship" (a bit of jargon for becoming lovers). After dinner, over brandy, Sid asked, "So what do you do, Rosa?"

Rosa, always eager to explain her work, said, "I'm a sociologist at the Waggoner Institute."

"No kidding?" Sid, a salesman for IBM, is impressed. He likes smart women. His first wife never moved from in front of the TV set. So he and Rosa plunge into a discussion of her work, but after fifteen minutes Sid is groggy. He simply can't "get a handle" on what Rosa is saying. After another fifteen minutes his interest has waned, and with a vague excuse he drifts back to the kitchen, where two of the men are discussing the World Series. Both Rosa and Sid, in the jargon of today's generation, "blew it."

How? Rosa, by thinking her professional jargon could pass as normal communication, and Sid, by not being honest enough to come out and say, "I don't understand what you mean."

To Rosa, no two things in her profession were ever alike. They were *isomorphic*. Different things were *allotropic*. She never divided things; she would *dichotomize* or *bifurcate* them. She saw her clients as *ego-integrated* or *action-oriented*. She even told Sid that she herself was *"oriented toward improvement of her ego-gratification-deprivation balance."*

So Sid split. How could he know she meant her *pleasure principle?* He was out to gratify his own. Poor Sid and poor Rosa. The physical was all there, but the metacommunication was all wrong.

One trouble with jargon is that helpful as it may be—another sociologist could have flung back book and text at Rosa—it carries a confusing metamessage to the uninitiated. It says, *I am boastful, boring, and pompous*. To the initiated, it says, *I have sat at the feet of the same masters and absorbed the same lessons*.

What Sid objected to in Rosa was not so much the use of jargon as the emotional state the jargon induced in him. Listening to her he felt inferior, ignorant, and stupid—and yet he himself had listened to and used equally pretentious jargon, and had been satisfied with it.

At a recent opening of the work of a new painter, Sid discussed art with a close friend and talked of the painter's *nativist impulse,* suggesting he belonged to a movement of *national self-definition,* and when the talk turned to architecture, he nodded, engrossed, as his friend labeled today's good architecture an *interpretive tool of a creative act* breaking with the *constraints of doctrinaire modernism,* but always within the *socioeconomic context.*

The jargon Sid was familiar with flowed easily, and while it was just as pretentious as Rosa's, it sent different metasignals to Sid. *You are intelligent and bright,* it said. *You know all the proper attitudes to art.*

The sound of the words, the rolling syllables of phrases like *doctrinaire modernism,* did the trick. The meaning of the phrase, of all the phrases Sid and his friend used, was unimportant. What was important to them were the metasignals that told each he belonged to the "in" crowd.

VERBAL INFLATION

In all jargon, the metasignals are of prime importance. Consider the doctor who tells a harried mother that her child might have trouble with deglutition. It would take a bit of guts for her to pin him down and discover that deglutition is swallowing. Usually the metasignals that accompany the "big words" are so frightening that the mother is afraid to question the statement. She doesn't really want to understand what the problem is. She just wants to hear something in the doctor's voice, an absolute self-assurance, that will put her fears to rest. The signal she reads is *Your child is very sick but he's in good hands . . . the very best hands!* Thank God, she sighs. I can relax and trust the doctor.

In many cases the doctor is not aware of what he's doing. He uses jargon unconsciously because he has been trained to think in medical jargon. But there are times when the jargon is deliberately used to impress the gullible layman. As long ago as the thirteenth century, the medieval physician Arnold of Villanova suggested that his contemporary physicians use jargon when they were unable to make a definite diagnosis. Tell the patient that he has an obstruction of the liver, he advised, and use the word obstruction because they do not know what it means.

Not only will the patient fail to understand, he might have added, but he won't want to understand. Behind the jargon is a disturbing metasignal: *There is something very wrong with you.*

The metamessages may work the same way with all medical jargon. You feel more helpless with cholelithiasis than with gallstones. You can deal with a headache, but cephalgia is a frightening symptom. Any woman can accept menstrual problems, but dysmenorrhea is hard to take.

One woman we know handled the jargon problem very well. After an examination, her orthopedist solemnly told her that she had acute tendonitis. Refusing to let his metasignals frighten her, she said, "Now tell it to me in basic English, Doc. What's the matter?"

He relaxed and told her she had tennis elbow, and she drew a sigh of relief. That was something she could deal with. "But the interesting part," she told us later, "is that when he said tennis elbow, there was none of that *I am God* in his voice. He was matter of fact and down to earth." In short, his metacommunication fit the diagnosis.

But one final word about medical jargon. It isn't always bad. A woman with an operable cancer of the uterus was able to handle it because her doctor told her she had a neoplasm. It wasn't until after successful surgery that she learned that her neoplasm was cancer. Another man just out of intensive care fought his way back to health comforted by the belief that a coronary occlusion wasn't as bad as a heart attack.

Very often medical jargon can mask the seriousness of a disease at a time when the patient is unable to deal with his problem. Then the doctor's metamessage, *I am supremely competent. Trust me,* does more good than harm.

As common as jargon is in medicine, it is even more so in education. Any journal on the subject is overwhelmingly obscure and circumlocutious—and the jargon filters down to the educators themselves, even on the grammar-school level. Let's eavesdrop on a meeting between Mrs. Lopez and her son's teacher. Mrs. Lopez is rightly concerned about Rafael's education, and she can't understand why the teacher has him reading about Dick and Jane while the boy next to him is on David Copperfield.

"We are implementing a program of individualized instruction. Rafael is reading at his natural level."

Mrs. Lopez is confused, but she is a smart woman. She cuts through the metacommunication of the teacher's jargon. "Do you think my Rafael is slow?"

"None of our students is slow," the teacher answers primly. "The school's diagnostic prescription techniques placed Rafael at a certain level. His motivational input makes him happier without pressure."

"He doesn't seem happy," Mrs. Lopez says doubtfully. The metasignals behind the teacher's words seem to say, *We know better than you what's good for your son.*

"Maybe he should be in a group-paced classroom, oriented to his special needs," the teacher says thoughtfully. "It could be implemented within the framework of individualization. . . ."

This is too much. Mrs. Lopez knows when she is licked. She also knows her son, Rafael, is a bright boy. If the school knows this too, perhaps she shouldn't persist. All the confusing terms do not make sense to her, but they give the impression that something important is going on. Their metasignals tell her to relax. Rafael will make it!

Mrs. Lopez was manipulated by the use of jargon, and that manipulative effect can be used in almost any walk of life. It's particularly effective in that common, everyday situation, trouble with the car.

Dad comes in stomping the snow from his feet. "The goddamned motor won't turn over! Can you get the garage on the phone?"

The car is towed in, and that evening dear old Dad goes to the garage to find out the damages. As he staggers back, bill in hand, he asks weakly, "What was wrong?"

Now comes the metasmokescreen to keep him reeling. "You ain't got enough voltage to your solenoid," the mechanic tells him sadly, chewing on a toothpick.

The careful juxtaposition of *ain't* with the technical jargon convinces Dad that the mechanic is honest, down to earth. The toothpick helps.

"What does that mean?" he asks helplessly.

"Well—you can't compress the Bendix spring, and that don't let the engaging lever release the armature."

"It's that bad?"

"Worse." Most mechanics are merciful enough to

stop right there, but this one sees the weakening effect on Dad and moves in for the kill. "The exciter winding don't turn the pinion against the flywheel, and there ain't sufficient torque to the crankshaft."

There are beads of sweat on Dad's forehead as he writes out the check for thirty dollars, figuring he got off easy. He'll never know that the only work the mechanic did was to charge his dead battery!

OF POLITICS AND ADS

Politics, as we noted before, is another area where jargon can be troweled over the most blatant cracks in the economic façade. A statement in political jargon can send a comforting metamessage even though the facts behind the statement are alarming. Words such as *inflation* or *deficit financing* make the electorate uneasy. They send out a metamessage of fear. A canny political speaker avoids them and uses phrases like *public works* and *tax relief* instead. These are comfortable words, and you think of new schools and hospitals and more money for everyone when you hear them. The U.S. Senate gets into the same act by calling its recess a *nonlegislative period*, and the House, not to be outdone, comes up with a *district work period* for its recess.

Boom and bust is another phrase that arouses uneasiness, but change the jargon and call it a *normalizing business cycle* with *rolling readjustments* and you can hear it and still be relaxed. The metasignals come across as *All's well. All is as it should be*.

The stock market no longer *plunges* in the speeches of these wise politicians. It goes into a *technical correction*. *Plunge* is a desperate word. It reminds us of the bankers and brokers during the Depression who took the twenty-story plunge. But *technical correction* is very satisfying, very reassuring. So is that other bit of economic jargon, *preparing the base for a new rise*.

There is a constant hunt among political speech writers for happier terms than depression and inflation. Both arouse so much apprehension among voters that they may want to send in a whole new team if they're threatened with either. *Depression* has been changed to *recession*, a term not quite as frightening, or even to a *healthy cutback*, which gives us the feeling that something good is happening.

The latest attempt to change the metasignals in inflation has been the coined word *stagflation*, a word so hard to visualize that most people simply accept it without much emotional turmoil. Anything that sounds stagnant can't be too bad in inflationary terms, or can it?

The *military-industrial complex* had a frightening sound when we read about its activities. There is something ominous about the term *complex*. It signals a devious quality. By substituting *community* for *complex*, a completely different metamessage was sent out. The *military-industrial community* is quite a different thing. It has a pleasant, neighborly metasignal to it. It works to reassure us.

While we're on the subject of military jargon, it's good to learn that the Pentagon won the Overall 1977 Doublespeak Award from the National Council of Teachers of English for calling the neutron bomb a *radiation-enhancement weapon*. The CIA won a runner-up award for calling its experiments in human behavioral control the Society for the Investigation of Human Ecology!

Advertisers, like politicians, know the value of manipulative metacommunication. Listen to the Yankee drawl of a huckster on television pushing *home-baked* bread. Do any of us seriously believe it's not made in a factory. It doesn't matter. We put the intellect aside and ride with the emotions, with the metamessage behind home-baked. We also fall for the metasignal of his drawl, and we visualize steaming loaves coming out of a wood-burning oven. Or we watch an actress such as Margaret Hamilton serving coffee in an old-fashioned country store with the additional metasignal of an old-fashioned name like Cora.

In both commercials we're dealing with nostalgia for the days when everything was supposed to taste better. The viewer is seduced not only by the picture but by Cora's crusty delivery. Her voice sends the metasignals of a loving old aunt-mother-grandmother who wants only the best for you.

In addition to the metasignals around the words, the voice patterns and the backgrounds, there are the words themselves. The copywriters never give up the search for some magical phrase that will evoke a burning desire to run out and buy their product.

In car commercials, Dodge advertises a *luxurious* compact. AMC, not to be outdone, describes a *new-sized personal* car (two metasignals in one), while Oldsmobile appeals to the snob with *sophisticated sport*.

Spotting the metasignals in advertising is a great game, and it may help you to brush away the obscuring cloud from the product. Here are a few more picked at random from home magazines. In floors, the *richness* of color. In perfume, the *experience* of Masumi. *Classic* furniture, *legendary* furs, the *ultimate* cigar, the *costliest* perfume, the *classic* fragrance for men, and in jeans, Levi pushes *body language* for men.

Since the organic revolution, the nation's cereals have leaped into the metafield. Some are advertised as *naturally* sweetened and on the list of contents we see sugar. Well, sugar is natural, but why make the distinction? Because *natural* has an honest metamessage behind it, *natural* goodness, *natural* ingredients, *natural* taste and flavor. It carries us back to the time when food was made by hand in primitive kitchens. We attach the value judgment of good to all such food, just as we do to *handmade* clothes and *hand-craftd* furniture. *Crafted* arouses a different image from *made*. It reminds us of a craftsman, a man who knows and loves his trade, not just a carpenter—the furniture must be better if it's *hand-crafted*.

THE LAID-BACK LINGO

Jargon exists on so many levels that often we tend to forget that it's jargon. Eventually it merges, imperceptibly, into slang. Today's young people have a slang-jargon of their own. A friend tried for acceptance from her twelve-year-old son by telling him she thought his haircut was "real cool."

Her son looked at her in a pained way and said, "Mom, please tell me my hair looks nice, but don't say cool! Especially," he added as an afterthought, "around my friends!"

The idea of his mother using the jargon of his own age group annoyed him. It sounded wrong, and he knew his friends would laugh. But most important, it did away with a valuable function of jargon, exclusivity.

The young often use jargon, *it's cool, it's tough, it sucks* to exclude their elders as well as to form a common bond among themselves. The metasignals behind the slang cue them in to each other. They become recognition signals. The message they get from their friends is *I'm one of you*. The message they hear in their parents' use of the words is *I want to be one of you*, an obvious impossibility.

The moral: stick to your own generation.

In most cases the jargon is used by the young as a sort of shorthand, or shortspeak. It lets the user avoid any full explanation of ideas and feelings. It gives a false sense of the profound to shallow platitudes.

Cyra McFadden, a former English teacher turned author, gave an amusing example of this in an article in the *New York Times* magazine section.

"I can't get behind school right now," a failing student told her. "I'm not into Fs, and anyway, I don't think you ought to lay that authority trip on me. I mean, failing someone—wow, that's a value judgment."

Pressed about his failure to report on a Ray Bradbury story, he explained, "I can't relate to the dude."

"Do you mean you weren't interested in his ideas?" she asked. "You didn't find them sympathetic? Were you bored? Did you have trouble following the action?"

"Actually, I didn't exactly read it."

"For God's sake," she asked, "how do you know you didn't like it?"

Turning a serious gaze on her, he explained, "I just flashed on it."

Nothing in our culture separates the generations as much as this slang-jargon. The over-thirties can send the under twenties into laughter by using the jargon of their own youth. "Dad, nobody calls them reefers anymore and stop calling things snazzy!"

There is a vogue to jargon, and to be *with it* you have to use the right word at the right moment. Unfortunately the words fade fast. *Laid back* is on its way out, and so is *bummer*. *Gross*, as in "It was gross!" for something awful, or "It grossed me out!" lingers a while, but *the whole ball of wax* has dropped along the way, along with women described as *broads*, *dolls*, and *cuties*.

A *sexy woman* has changed to a *foxy lady*, and the metamessage has changed too. Sexy was Mae West and Betty Grable, Raquel Welch and Ann-Margret. Foxy is Pam Grier and Elke Sommer, Romy Schneider, a touch of the vixen, a sexual slyness.

In the last twenty years, the extraordinary proliferation of encounter groups, T groups, sensitivity training, self-help books, and emotional-awareness literature has produced a jargon of its own. This has infiltrated the language to produce a potpourri of professional terminology, street slang, and regional lingo used by everyone from preteens to mature lovers. You play scenes off the wall, go with the flow, do a number on someone, stay loose, dump on people, get into heavy trips, get your act together, and know where you're coming from.

Usually the jargon, with its pseudopsychiatric shorthand, lets you avoid intimacy by never getting below the ready phrases, but it can also be an emotional shortcut through the initial awkwardness of a first meeting.

Take a pleasant pickup in a neighborhood bar. Carl and Jean have been eyeing each other speculatively, and finally Carl takes his drink, moves over, and says, "This is a terrific place to hang out. I mean no one hassles you here."

Jean picks up the metasignals behind *terrific* and *hang out*. They define the generational group Carl belongs to. She agrees with, "I like it better than some of those yechy places downtown."

Yechy sends its own message to Carl. *I'm in the*

forefront. I know that gross is out, but yechy is still in.

After a few minutes they're on a first-name basis, and a short time later they launch into an intimate conversation. Carl explains that he has just gone through "a regressive period," and to Jean *regressive* means more than moving backward. It means that Carl is involved with therapy of some sort. She also picks up the pitch of his voice when he says regressive. It's flat, matter-of-fact, and sends a metasignal that says he's no longer in that stage.

Carl, sensing her interest and needing to talk, goes on. "My old lady and I were never really in touch with each other, like she was into her thing and I was into mine. We split."

Jean nods sympathetically. She gets the message. Carl was living with a woman, but it didn't work out. He's free now. The phrase *never really in touch,* with its sensitivity-training background, conveys loneliness and vulnerability. "I can dig that," Jean says in a low, sympathetic voice. "If you can't relate to someone, can't make contact, it's time to deep-six the whole affair."

"That's what I told myself." Carl is able to open up now. The sympathetic *I can dig* has a strong metamessage, stronger than *I can understand.* Dig goes deep, beneath the skin, beneath the emotions. *Deep-six* is also strong, stronger than ending or breaking up an affair. It implies a more drastic solution. The whole thing is finished, drowned, six fathoms down!

Carl goes on. "And the rejection bit! I went that route. I don't need that kind of grief."

"Rejection! That's the pits," Jean agrees, and the two of them are off and running.

What matters here is not only the metameaning behind the choice of jargon but also the fact that each is familiar with the other's jargon. Rejection has its dictionary meaning to most of us, but to those who, like Carl and Jean, have traveled the sensitivity-encounter route, rejection has many other connotations. The very sound of it calls up guilt, loneliness, selfishness, and a lack of understanding, so many qualities that enter into a relationship ending in rejection. It becomes a loaded word in metacommunication.

Most jargon consists of similarly loaded words. Take any intellectual cocktail party in any big city. Drift around and, between the hors d'oeuvres, listen to the jargon. Remember, its prime function is to send out the metasignals *I am important. I am knowledgeable. I am an expert in this or that field.*

In art talk, a subtle shift in meaning can be given to any word by using a suffix or prefix. *Neo-* and *-ism* are great ones. Neorealism, neosensorialism, neoimpressionism. A picture, a novel, a play, or a movie can be characterized by these labels, or, if you aren't comfortable with *neo-* and *-ism,* you can always class the work as *gripping,* or call it an *experience,* immediate, provocative—even absolute.

Among the favorite terms for throwing up an intellectual metasmokescreen in the current cocktail circuit are *ethos, decadent, perceptive, evocative, organic, plastic, existential, ambivalent.*

If you wish to use a few foreign phrases, try *mystique* or *kitsch.* If you want to capture the modern touch and show you're "with it," try *camp, a happening, turned on,* or *now,* as in the *now generation, kinky, funky* and even *it's the pits!*

At any intellectual cocktail party, if you expect to be *in,* you must start with the right greeting, using the correct jargon to address people. Even when you know their names, it's often a mistake to use them. Oddly enough, the metasignals behind feminine terms of endearment can indicate just how *in* you are. You can call a man *sweetie* or *doll* or *honey*, if you're a woman. If you're a man, you can use the same greetings for a woman, but another man is a *sweet guy*, or a *beautiful person*, or you can call him *baby*, or even *luv*. Luv can be used by men or women to men or women.

In all of these, the metamessage is instant intimacy. You are telling the other person, *I know you well enough to use a term of endearment*. But if you use such a term to someone you don't know, and he knows you don't know him, the message changes to *I really can't bother to get to know you*. It's enough to play the instant intimacy game, pretending an understanding and closeness that exists only in words of endearment.

THE USE OF EUPHEMISMS

"There are two things that drive me up the wall," a friend said recently. "One is the telephone company, and the other the tax people."

"So what else is new?"

"No, I don't mean what they do," he went on earnestly. "That's bad enough, but it's a matter of naming themselves. Now you take Information. At least what used to be called Information. When I wanted a number, I called Information. I felt they were doing what they had to do so I could pay to use their machines. Now what do I get? *Directory Service*. Some smartass PR guy got them to change the name in order to give me the feeling that they were doing me a favor."

"I see what you mean."

"And the tax people. Where do they come off changing the Internal Revenue Bureau to the Internal Revenue Service? Who's doing us a service?"

What our friend was protesting so bitterly was the professional use of euphemisms by both these institutions to change people's attitudes toward them, to influence the way the public saw them, or, in terms of metacommunication, to change the metamessage they were sending out. We hear the word *bureau* and we make an instant connection with bureaucracy and red tape, with inefficiency and frustration. How much better to hear *service* and make the natural connection with help, doing a favor, caring. Service is a very clever euphemism for bureau, and for information.

A euphemism is first cousin to jargon, even though its definition is quite different. Webster defines it as a pleasant word to replace an unpleasant one, but who is to judge what is pleasant and what unpleasant? Most people respond in the same way to the same words, but still, any two people *may* react in opposite fashion to the same metasignal. What is pleasant to one can offend the other.

Some cultures are very casual about body waste and sex. They look on both as normal, natural functions and make no fuss about either. But in our society, the parts of the body that produce waste or are involved with sex make us uneasy when they are mentioned. So much so that they are rarely called by their proper names. It all started with Victorian England, where women didn't even have legs because a man might be sexually aroused by legs. Instead they had limbs. Urination, defecation, and sex were rarely mentioned directly.

To a big extent, we're still under those old Victorian prohibitions. We are not comfortable with the sound of the real thing and so we turn to euphemisms. I wrote sex in the sentence before, and sex is a euphemism—for what? Our language has no good term for it. The old-fashioned fucking is too harsh for most of us. The medical coitus is too clinical. The slang, screwing, is too vulgar. Making love is too vague—and so we use sex, or a dozen other phrases, some coy, some funny, and some ugly, from *light my fire* to *making out, getting laid, getting it on, a roll in the hay, nookie, a piece of ass,* and even *it*. "All he cares about is it!"

For some, the metamessage behind the euphemism is ugly, and for some it is soft and dreamy. *Making love* has a tender metamessage while *a piece of ass* has a crude, harsh one. Sometimes the euphemism for sex is a very private one between lovers. It is their intimate secret and the metamessage is secrecy.

As for our other body functions, we never defecate. We make a BM or number two when we are children, and as we get older we go to the john or the head while our British cousins use the WC or the loo. Instead of urinating we make pee-pee, wee-wee, tinkle, number one, pish, we take a leak or pass our water. In each case the metamessage is either overpolite or overhostile. And where do we go for all these body functions? The variety of euphemisms for that private place boggles the imagination. There is really no proper word for it. Rest room? Do we rest there? Toilet? That comes from the French and means a little piece of cloth. Is it a lounge, a cloakroom, a men's room, a ladies' room, or, as the extra-cute diners have it, Moms and Dads?

We teach our children euphemisms for these things, and along with the euphemisms the child learns that there is something "dirty" about urinating and defecating, about sex and all the organs involved with it. He learns the euphemisms for the organs and actions, and somehow they soften the meaning. Each family develops its own set of nicknames, sometimes so unique that when a group of children get together they have a confusing number of different names for the same body function. In one family boom-booms are breasts, in another, bowel movements, and in a third the noise of a drum.

I know a girls' camp where use of the word *ass*, as in *you silly ass* or *get off your ass!* became a problem. The director, to overcome it, started a contest for an acceptable word for buttocks. The winner submitted *beholyabockel*, weird and inoffensive enough to send a metamessage of plain silliness.

Children, in spite of the euphemisms, begin using them to curse with. A nursery-school child, in anger, will call another a *BM* or a *Dutyhead*, and in doing so foreshadows the adult who uses anatomy and waste products as curses: *you shithead, you asshole, you prick, you cunt*. The metamessages behind all these words are rooted in the society's view of sex and defecation. The shock we get when we hear them is a shock only because they have been kept secret.

The metamessage from these words varies from person to person. In the United States a man who is called a prick is no good, mean, and a double-dealer. In America's Jewish subculture, a schmuck, the Jewish word for penis, is not the same as a prick. He's a dope, a fool, and a fall guy. The different metamessages can be traced to differences in the two cultures.

Culture gives the metamessage to the words, and this is particularly true of euphemisms. They may send one message in the white culture, another in the black, and still another in the Puerto Rican or Indian. A famous black TV comic used a one-liner based on just this principle. With a perfectly straight face, he told the audience, "I don't like to call a spade a spade. . . ."

The audience, after a shocked moment, burst into laughter. The metasignals behind spade were just confused enough to make the joke work.

FROM BIRTH TO DEATH

Sometimes we forget how pervasive euphemisms are in our lives. They are with us from birth to death. Thirty years ago, pregnant was a forbidden word. The play *The Moon Is Blue* shocked all of Broadway when the heroine used it on stage. Since the sexual revolution, it has become acceptable, but still, in most of America, pregnant women are *that way, expectant, knocked up, heavy with child,* or *enceinte*. Each has its own metamessage, none as exact as pregnant. *That way* signals indirection, vagueness; *expectant* adds to the secrecy of it. *Knocked up* sends a crude, contemptuous message, something done to a woman against her will. *Heavy with child* is old-fashioned, and it's a burden before it's even born, and *enceinte* is all too delicate to mention in English.

Giving birth is not much better. *Delivered* is less threatening. After all, packages and surprises are delivered.

When the girl grows up and reaches puberty she menstruates—or does she? You don't menstruate in polite society. A woman *falls off the roof,* a disaster, or it's *that time of month,* a big secret, or she has the *curse*. Women are cursed with this, or it may send out an even older metasignal: women are witches and cursed because of it. Perhaps she's *unwell*—menstruation is not healthy. It's a sickness. How much of a young woman's fear of menstruation and pregnancy are conditioned by these metamessages?

Even marriage has its euphemisms. *Tying the knot*. Prisoners are tied up. *Getting hitched*. This dates back to when oxen were hitched together to pull a plow—pulling together through life. *Hooked*. This suggests a fishing game with the man as the catch.

Divorce becomes *breaking up*, like an ice jam breaking on a frozen river, coming apart emotionally. *Splitting* has a harsher message, almost painful, and today's touch, *it's Splitsville*, is more flip, less personal, a place, not a state, and it comes across without any deeply felt emotion.

In later years there is the *senior citizen* instead of old men and women. Seniors are always superior, established. You might add that seniors also graduate, but in this case it's not worth asking, Where to?

And so it goes from life to death. Now there's a word, *death!* We shiver at the metamessages behind death and dying. We always have and probably always will because death itself is so bewildering and terrifying a concept that most of us simply cannot face.

And because death is so frightening, and the metasignal of the word so awful, we substitute *passing away*, or *passing on*. *He left us, he's gone*. The euphemisms soften the impact. The dead one is somewhere else, they say, not here, but *somewhere*.

If you really want a handful of good euphemisms about death and dying, stop in at any funeral home and talk to one of the salesmen, or better still, read Jessica Mitford's *The American Way of Death*. There are no undertakers anymore. There are *morticians* or *funeral directors* or even *grief therapists*. Coffins have become *caskets*, hearses *coaches*, bodies are *loved ones*, and cremated ashes are *remains*. The funeral parlor has become a *slumber room*, a *reposing room*, or even a *chapel*. The metamessage here is *holy*.

Along with death, murder sends a frightening metasignal. A current euphemism for murder is *waste*. Criminals will speak of *wasting a man*. The implication is that the man is useless, something to be thrown out. It takes the act of murder away from reality, but we've always had a load of euphemisms for murder. Gangsters took victims *for a ride, bumped them off, wiped them out*.

Another area where euphemisms abound is the job world. No one is fired anymore. You're *laid off, let go*, or the firm has to *cut back*. Many businesses do this out of mixed motives. It is easier on the employee, they claim, to get the *fired* message in euphemistic terms. It softens the blow and he doesn't feel the same sense of defeat he would in being fired. But in fact perhaps the worker would do better knowing the truth. The euphemisms give him a sense of unfinished business. He doesn't know where he stands.

But it is also easier for the employer to use the euphemisms. He isn't quite as much of a villain to himself if he lays a man off instead of firing him. The entire act of being laid off gives a metamessage that it's out of everyone's hands. It's a function of the business itself.

Once we begin to examine our speech for jargon and euphemisms, we become aware that every aspect of life is crowded with them, and more are being added all the time. In fact, we can begin to wonder if we could really get along without them. Science certainly seems unable to. In defense, scientists protest that such jargon becomes a shorthand that makes it easier to get difficult ideas across.

Scientific jargon is indeed a shorthand, but while it can help to explain difficult ideas, it can also make simple and basic ideas difficult to understand and it can muddy up the intellectual waters. Sometimes, if the metasignals are right, it can make a simple idea sound complex.

In understanding the true purpose behind the use of euphemisms and jargon, we must understand what the words convey to us, what the metamessage is regardless of its real meaning. The semanticist traces words to their original meanings. He will, for example, consider the word *fink* in its meaning as an informer and perhaps trace it to the Scandinavian for the word finch, a person who sings to the police.

The metasemanticist (to coin our own bit of jargon) is more intrigued with the sound of the word. What does fink sound like? It's a hard, ugly word, and we get an unpleasant meaning from it, from the sound of it, no matter what the true meaning or derivation.

A Los Angeles economist, Arthur H. Hawkins, writing on labor-management relations, seems very aware of the metamessages behind so many words. He suggests euphemisms to overcome these messages. *Labor,* he notes, has historical overtones of manual toil. Most people we class as labor have nothing to do with such toil. Instead of labor, he offers *paycheck population*. It takes all the sting (and strength) out of the word.

He has a few other goodies. *Cease to purchase* for boycott. *Motivation through fear* for coercion, *request* for demand, *difference* for dispute, *temporary work cessation* for layoff, *distinction without evaluation* for segregation, and a real winner, *substitute noncertified worker,* for scab. He is sure that a rose by any other name would smell much sweeter.

Whether his system works or not, it gets to the basic fact that some words are easier to accept than others. Some words upset us while others soothe us. Some words we consider beautiful while others sound ugly. *Dawn, moon, heart, shadow, hush, murmur, lumi-*

nous are all considered beautiful words. *Crunch, gripe, fink, flatulant, cacophony, spinach* are all classed as ugly.

Sometimes it is sound alone that determines the beauty or ugliness of a word, and sometimes it is association. Sometimes, one man's beautiful word is another's ugly one. But the important point is that every word has some sort of metamessage attached to it. The message may be from our own personal background, or from the society, but using that word will send out a message over and beyond its true meaning.

5

Station Identification

GREAT EXPECTATIONS

In a study of educational techniques, a teacher was told that her new class were all gifted children. "You should get above-average results from them," she was advised, and by the end of the term she was getting just that, better than average work.

The remarkable thing about it all was that in reality the class was not unusual. They were just an average group of students with IQs within the normal range. The teacher had been deceived about their potential.

This study uncovered many answers to many questions about teaching and children, but it left even more questions unanswered. One point it did make with unusual clarity is that a child will usually live up to a teacher's expectations when the child believes those expectations are honest.

An unanswered question was, In what way did the teacher communicate to the students that they were special and could do superior work? She didn't tell them that in so many words, but obviously something about her attitude convinced the students that they were gifted.

Further studies showed that the special "something" in the teacher's attitude was, in part, the type of work she gave the class, and in part how she presented it. But the strongest "something" was the teacher herself and her attitude toward the class and toward their ability.

There was an extra amount of confidence and interest in her voice that said, "You're bright children." There was a constant reassuring tone that told them they would do well, very well. The children picked up these metasignals and reacted positively to them.

When a student's work did not measure up to the teacher's expectations, as often happened, the student was not treated with disappointment, anger, or annoyance. Instead, the teacher assumed that this was an exception, an accident, a bad day, a momentary slip—and the student believed her and felt reassured. The next time around, he tried harder, determined to live up to what the teacher knew he could do.

The exact metacommunication that tells a child, "I expect the best," is difficult to pinpoint. In part it consists of a level tonal assurance, a lack of verbal impatience, an absence of irony, sarcasm, put-downs, irritation, and a dozen other negative qualities. The teacher who expects the best asks her questions with conviction, knowing the answers she gets will be right, and the child picks up that conviction.

Most of this is transmitted through the voice, but a surprising amount is in the attitude, in touch, and in facial expression.

An experiment similar to the one done with "gifted" children was done with "gifted" mice. A scientist was given a group of ordinary mice, but told that they were a special breed, trained to run a maze in record time.

Working with these mice, the unwary scientist found that they did learn faster than other mice and did run the maze more quickly.

But mice know nothing of our language. How was the scientist able to communicate his expectations to them? An examination of all the variables in the test concluded that the unusually good results were due to the way he had handled the mice, the way he talked to them, the metacommunication in his voice, the tone, the confidence, the reassurance, and the certainty. They absorbed all the messages and performed accordingly!

LABELING

In a broader view of both these experiments, the teacher and the scientist used a principle common to all societies at all levels—the principle of labeling. All our expectations are prejudiced, and we have very different expectations for different people, even on a national level. We think of people in terms of national characteristics. We expect Americans to be *mercenary*, after the big buck, and we label them that way in our minds. We label Germans *neat* and *orderly*, English *cold*, *distant*, and *reserved*, Italians *emotional*, Japanese *polite*—and so it goes. We pin a very narrow label on a very broad, far from homogeneous group. We do it on racial levels too. Blacks are *musical*, Indians are *stoic*, Orientals *inscrutable*. We even label the sexes—men are *aggressive*, women *passive*.

On a family basis, the labels are sometimes attached by the neighbors. "Those Joneses are trash . . . always on welfare." Or the label may be attached by the family itself. "We Smiths would rather go hungry than ask for government help!" The Smith boy, growing up with this label of awesome independence, lives up to it as readily as the Jones girl lives up to her label. "They all think we're trash? I'll act like trash!"

The label may be less inclusive, even sexist. "The men in our family are always professionals." When Bill finds that carpentry is the work he loves best, he faces a family conflict—and a conflict with himself. His inner strength may allow him to go through with his own desires and become a carpenter, but then he knows that he hasn't lived up to the family label and he goes through life with a sense of guilt. He may even create his own label. "I'm a failure, really." It doesn't matter that Bill is a success in his field, that in time he owns his own business and makes more money than his brother Bob, who became a lawyer. Bill is still not a professional man, and his inner label still reads *failure*.

Labeling within a family starts very early. Before the baby understands verbal language, he responds to body language and metacommunication. He senses the love in his parents' voice before he understands the words, and he also senses the rejection, indifference, fear, or hostility, and he reacts to those emotions too.

If he's treated with love and gentleness, he responds with both emotions. Later, when he understands speech, he accepts his label. Jimmy is the *nice* one in the family, or Sally, who's been a colicky baby, earns the label of *troublemaker*. Each child, along with his given name, picks up a label. She's the *clever* one. He's the *pushy* one. Norman is always late. Betty is so hard to love. Barbara is cold. George marches to a different drum. Jack is wild. Natalie is sweet, and so on. The labels may reflect reality. Natalie may be sweet, but as often as not the reality has been imprinted on the child by the label. If Natalie hears that she is sweet often enough, she begins to act sweet. You tend to live up to your label.

The students in the teaching experiment were labeled *bright*, and they managed to be bright, to work beyond their ordinary ability. But if this is so, isn't labeling sometimes a good thing? If the newspapers label a statesman a peacemaker, won't he try to become one in truth? If he's labeled decent, honest, a champion of human rights, won't he try to live up to those flattering labels? If a child is labeled good, smart, happy—won't she also try to become all of those things?

The answer, of course, is obvious. No matter how much a person is influenced for good by labeling, in essence the label takes away his free will. No child is always good, and if he tries to live up to the *good* label, he must suppress the very normal times when he is bad, mischievous, angry, contrary, or sullen. In his own mind he loses his right to be any of those things. Everyone points out that good boys aren't like that. He tries to become a good boy and push down all the healthy reactions of childhood.

In time, like hidden acid, such suppressed feelings can eat away at his heart, or sometimes explode into violence, unexpected and bewildering. The good boy suddenly goes bad.

THE IMPOSSIBLE DREAM

There are times when a label can be destructive because it is simply impossible to live up to. Friends of ours with a teenage son gave him the label *genius* early in the game.

"Charles is so gifted, he frightens me sometimes," his father would tell us in front of him, showing us a perfectly ordinary sketch the boy had made. When Charles gave up art and went into music, his father was just as excited, just as convinced of his genius. "Charles is writing a fantastic composition," he told us, awestruck. "His teacher thinks it's truly remarkable . . ." and when Charles gave up music for writing, he was almost the equal of Hemingway.

It was clear that poor Charles was turning desperately from one field to another, twisting and turning to escape his father's lavish labeling. He knew the truth about his own abilities and he knew his limits and knew also that he could never live up to the label his father had given him.

In the end he dropped out of school and the last we heard had joined a commune out West. "Charles is simply incredible at meditation," his father told us the last time we saw him. "You wouldn't believe his control!"

The inability to live up to someone else's improbable dream can occur all through life, not just in childhood, and it is almost always a destructive force. In a marriage a husband may label his wife a wonderful homemaker, a perfect mother, an understanding wife when she is none of these things. The metamessage she receives from the label is not *You are wonderful*, but *I see you as someone with capabilities beyond those you have*, and, more deadly, *Unless you measure up to my expectations, I can't love you*. The double bind of these two messages can crack a marriage wide open!

The impossible-dream label can just as easily be given to a husband by a wife. *Tom is a great provider. Dick is such a terrific father. Harry is a perfect lover!*

Unrealistic labeling exists in all parts of life, in families, among lovers, between friends, and even at work. In a job situation, expecting results beyond his capabilities can frustrate an employee and eventually make him produce below his ability. A certain amount of encouragement, however, will usually produce excellent work.

In the teaching experiment, the teacher's expectations were not beyond the class's capabilities. The most important factor was the teacher's conviction that the students could and would do the work. It was an honest conviction, and that honesty was transmitted to the students. She believed in them and they worked to justify her belief.

When the expectations are false, the labeling done in sarcasm or contempt, the metasignals around the message give away the truth. The wife says of her husband, "John's a great father." The label can be given in sincerity, and John, hearing it often enough, may try to live up to his wife's honest expectations. But if the label is given dishonestly, the metamessage of *false* is picked up by John. This false label, like the unrealistic one, can become destructive. John may well give up any further attempts at fathering.

Another label, essentially destructive, can be given indirectly.

"Here. Let me do it the right way," the father says, taking the job away from the child. The label: *incompetent*.

"How can a smart student like you hand in such a dumb paper?" the teacher asks. The label: *stupid*.

The lover says, "Other women seem to respond without any trouble." The label: *frigid*.

In each case an unspoken label is pinned to the person. The pinning may be denied. "I never meant that!" but still it becomes an effective moment of truth to the person who hears it. The child knows he's incompetent. The student knows he's stupid and the lover knows she's frigid.

NICKNAMES

Sometimes a label is pinned on a person in the form of a nickname. Children are called Red, Shorty, Sandy, Dusty, Egghead—and each nickname calls up a mental image that sticks with the child. Perhaps nicknames are helpful. The boy labeled Butch can have his ego stroked a bit by the masculinity of the name even as a girl called Beauty or Angel by her father preens her feminine feathers. But this is the rare case. Too often nicknames are cruel and hurt.

At a recent business convention, a friend of ours met someone from his childhood and greeted him with, "My God, Squeak! I haven't seen you in years." Then they both stood there, embarrassed and awkward. Later, he told us, "Squeak was a nickname from the years when his voice was changing. He was a thin, gangly kid then, a squeak of a kid, and the name fit. Now he's a huge six-footer with a deep bass!"

He went on to tell us that the nickname had been given at a summer camp. "Looking back, I think there were some very cruel counselors there who labeled all of us. One kid was called Blubber all summer because he cried the first day. Another was Eppi, short for epidemic. He was a bit of a plague. Blizzard marched to another drum. He had been lost in a blizzard. We called the male counselors Uncle, the women Aunt, but one woman counselor was nicknamed Uncle. Just that. She was businesslike, maybe a bit masculine in her manner, and plain. I never realized how cruel that label was, what it said about her before we even knew her—but it was hard as hell to know anyone past their nickname. I think, in a sense, we all lived up to those labels."

You don't have to go to summer camps or schools for nicknames. We were visiting friends one evening when neighbors, a husband and wife, dropped over. The husband kept talking about his *boss*. "The boss never liked the city, so we moved out here. The boss is crazy about Johnny Carson. The boss thinks I should cut down on my cholesterol."

Bemused at first, we thought he had found the ultimate in paternalistic jobs, but then we realized he was talking about his wife. His label for her, his pet nickname, was the Boss.

She seemed a quiet and unassuming woman, and after they left we asked our friends, "Does she really rule the roost in that family?"

"Not a bit. That's just his way of teasing her. In fact, if anyone calls the shots, he does. Right down the line."

After meeting them a few more times, we began to realize that his nickname for his wife sent out a metamessage of *You're in control* only on a superficial level. Underneath the kidding, he was saying *I resent whatever control you have and I'm going to rub your nose in it!* And below the resentment there seemed an even deeper resentment of the entire marriage.

The nicknames in a marriage, the labels husband and wife put on each other, are valuable clues to the suppressed feelings they have for each other, just as, in general, the nicknames men use for women—or women for men—give us valuable clues to their deeper feelings. She's my *ball-and-chain, my better half, the old lady, Himself, the Lord and Master* (with proper sarcasm), and she's a *cunt*, or he's a *prick* (with contempt and hostility).

We know a couple who split up recently after ten years of a hate-filled marriage, and in all those ten years they called each other nothing but *Sweetie* and *Dearie*. But listening to these "loving" labels, there was never any doubt of the venom behind them.

We also know a childless couple who call each other *Mom* and *Pop*, and though there is genuine love between them, they are just as hard to be with as the *Dearie, Sweetie* pair. What comes across is an unbearable yearning for the family they are denied, a loneliness and a longing for children. The messages behind the nicknames are as sad as the others are angry.

Checking your friends for their nicknames can be a fascinating parlor game. What does the nickname say, and how closely does it relate to the person? Oddly enough, many nicknames, even insulting ones, fill a need in the person who is labeled. A television show, "Lou Grant," built a charming incident around this point. A slovenly newspaper photographer is nicknamed *Animal*. At one stage when the characters decide to stop labeling each other, they begin to call him by his real name, Dennis. After a while he turns to the others and asks wistfully, "Don't you like me anymore?"

To the labeled one, the nickname, no matter how harsh, can spell affection and, above all, acceptance. We may use nicknames for people we dislike behind their backs, but we rarely use the names to their face. Using a nickname is an intimate gesture. It says, *You belong*.

In families *Mom* and *Pop* or *Dad* are almost universal nicknames, and in many families the first boy becomes *Brother*, the first girl *Sister*. A friend with three brothers and a sister swears he never knew his sister's real name until he was an adult. "She was just Sis to all of us."

What these family nicknames often do is lock the labeled ones into rigid roles where their own identity is submerged in their family function. You are a *Mom* first, a woman second, a *Dad* before a man, and a *Brother* or *Sister* before an individual. It insures a family togetherness, and it creates responsibility—whether the individual wants it or not.

THE LITTLE ONES

We often use diminutives in place of nicknames to label people. Charlie, Bobby, Trish, Annie all change the image of the person. What sort of a message does the name Jimmy Carter send that James never could? Jimmy could be the boy next door, amiable, honest, lovable—one of us. The total image, the casual clothes, the smile, the soft Southern accent, the hesitant speech is summed up in the name Jimmy.

James is too formal for the image. There is a distancing quality to James, a formality, a stiffness. The same is true of William as compared to Billy. The new career of the President's brother couldn't have happened to a William. It had to be a Billy.

The diminutive sends a metasignal of intimacy. Theodore Roosevelt's Teddy worked because he appealed, in an intimate way, to the entire nation. However, the diminutive wasn't possible with Franklin D. How improper Frankie would have been, even Frank! He needed the distancing quality of the full Franklin D.

We clung to John for President Kennedy, but easily

accepted Jackie for his wife. It seemed fitting that the wife should be closer to us, more intimate.

Diminutives tend to get lost as we mature. When grown children still call their parents Mommy and Daddy, it may well be a sign of immaturity, of wanting to be a child again. The daughter of a friend had grown from Mommy and Daddy to Mother and Dad. At twenty-three she left home and took an apartment of her own. When her first love affair broke off, she called home.

"I knew what had happened the moment I answered the phone," her father told us. "It was her first word, 'Daddy?' and I wanted to take her in my arms and comfort her."

As all of us grow up, Mommy changes to Mom or Mother while Daddy becomes Dad but rarely takes the final step to Father. If we progress beyond Dad, it's to the first name. Bill or Tom or whatever. We are fully grown.

Mother, however, rarely gets her own first name in a family. We need her too much as a mother. In those families where the children are raised to call their parents by their proper names, there is often a lesser degree of intimacy and a greater amount of independence. One young woman told us that the day she finished her analysis, her mother became Sue, her father Sam, "and I, after twenty-five years of Dotty, became Dorothy!"

A name, in essence, is the label we put on a person at birth, but birth seems a sorry time to label a human being. He is still too unformed, too amorphous. Certain primitive tribes wait until adolescence and even maturity to name their members, to give them their true names. By then their characters have been formed, and a name can be chosen to fit that character. It's different in our culture, and often the name becomes a rigid mold that the man or woman must grow into.

In the early melting-pot days, when each group clung to its roots and resisted assimilation, children were given ethnic names. Later, as they broke loose from their old-world cultures, they searched for American names. Even surnames were legally Americanized, and an attempt was made to blend into the WASP woodwork.

In more recent years, many ethnic groups are going back to the older names. The emergence of Israel as a country gave the Jews in America a sense of identity with the Hebrew culture, and the old Biblical names began to reappear, David and Rebecca and Rachel, Seth and Jonathan. The emerging African nations brought a rash of African names to American blacks. The metasignals behind the "funny, foreign names" changed, and they were no longer funny, but somehow proud and inspiring.

With names such as Joy, Hope, or Charity, a trait is set up and often expected. The child who fails to live up to her name may be troubled by an unconscious sense of inadequacy. The same troubling inadequacy can arise from the pride of a family name, even an ordinary one. John Smith the Third has the reputation of the First and Second to live up to.

EGO FEEDBACK

Labels can be pinned on others and on ourselves in dozens of ways, and sometimes, when others fail to label us, we do it ourselves. We drop and break a treasure and say, "I'm so stupid!" Rarely, "I did such a stupid thing."

The label sticks in our mind, *stupid*. We think a normal person can sometimes do a stupid thing, but a stupid person always does stupid things. It becomes a matter of living up to what's expected of us, and what we expect of ourselves. We send ourselves an ego metamessage, *I am stupid*. And that takes the responsibility for the action out of our hands.

Labels, like nicknames, tend to stick. The grown man who was called Squeak is not unique. Many of us have friends who still carry their childhood nicknames, Stretch, Slim, Rusty, Curley. Jessica Mitford writes of her own family growing to maturity with the nicknames Bobo, Deba, Decca. Her parents were always called Muv and Farve, her own child, Dinkey.

Often we accept our nicknames as our personalities. The child who's called Crazy Eddie by his friends takes pride in living up to his name, in doing all sorts of *crazy* things to win his friends' admiring "Wow! That Crazy Eddie'll do anything—anything!" There's a little bit of awe in their head-shaking evaluation, and it stokes the ego of Crazy Eddie. He is accepted, and even if that acceptance is negative, perhaps damaging in some way, it is still acceptance—one of the most important human needs.

When I was a child, there was a boy down the block whose nickname was Worms. Worms Fogarty! That's right. He ate them. How it had started, I don't know, but he'd gladly demonstrate his skill for an audience of more than two, and for reward he wanted nothing more than the disgust mixed with wonder on our faces. He earned his immortality on the block by his diet, but even after he outgrew his noxious habit he clung to the label. It singled him out and gave him a very special, if disgusting, uniqueness, one he needed and enjoyed.

Your nickname sends a signal to others, but it also

sends a signal to your own ego. It becomes a sort of metaidentity. The sound of your nickname is a summing up of your own persona. I know of a family who referred to their middle child as the monster. It started when he was just a baby, a big one and hyperactive. Why monster? "Because he was clumsy and always up to some monstrous trick," his parents explained. As he grew older and slowed down, the nickname clung and he lived up to it.

"It took us a few years to realize that we had played Frankenstein," his father told us. "Once we realized what we had created, we set out to change him."

"How?"

"We got some counseling help. It was suggested that we couldn't do it all in one fell swoop, so we did it in steps. We started calling him by his given name, Andrew or Andy. It's funny, but in less than a year he had undergone a personality change. He's a nice kid now. When he does something we used to call monstrous, we shrug and say, 'Growing pains.' We realize his old tricks were part of growing up a middle kid and fighting for attention. We had given him the right to misbehave. After all, what can a monster do but misbehave?"

And, they might have added, they had started a feedback to Andrew's ego. In his struggle for a sense of identity, he found recognition as a monster. Ordinary behavior was ignored, but monstrous stunts gained recognition. It was simple behavior modification.

Monster is a hostile label, but it carries a reluctant admiration for sheer perversity. Sometimes, however, family labels are given with nothing but hostility. It's a sad truth that not all parents love their children. Selma, when she was just a baby, was constantly referred to as the bitch. She wasn't called that to her face, but like Andrew's monster, it was used to talk about her, used by her brothers, her parents, and their friends. "What's the bitch been up to? Did you hear about the bitch's latest?"

Selma, like Andrew, knew her family label, and understood the metamessage behind it. She reacted accordingly. If being a bitch got that much attention, she'd go right on outbitching herself.

She carried her bitchiness right up to adulthood and into her relationships with men, and, saddest of all, into her marriage, which ended, predictably, in divorce.

An interesting thing about Selma is that she left home at nineteen to go to California and try to get into films. She changed her name and became moderately successful in a modeling career. She never returned home, nor did she remain in contact with her family. A typical bitchy trick, they decided, and wiped her out of their lives. Yet, somehow, Selma's *bitch* label went with her in spite of her name change. She let her lovers, and later her husband, know what she had been called, and they gladly took on the punishing role she offered them. They fed her the label that keyed her into the persona she knew she was.

BY THE RULES

There are rules for using nicknames, labels, and even proper names. Very hostile nicknames, *Monster* or *Bitch*, are rarely used face-to-face, only when talking about someone, but they may be used in the person's presence. Physical nicknames can be derisive—Fatty, Baldy, Skinny—and if so they're rarely used by friends face-to-face. But they can also be admiring—

Blondy, Muscles—or positive—Big Boy, Beautiful—and then they are used face-to-face. Personality nicknames such as Wacko or Stud may be derisive, but they are not only used face-to-face, but often demanded by the nicknamee. "Call me Stud. . . ."

In the use of given names, there is a peculiar status mechanism at work. A child rarely calls an adult by his first name without the honorific Mr. or Mrs., or Uncle or Aunt for close family friends. The adult, on the other hand, is allowed to call any child by his proper name or nickname.

Even among adults the status game holds. If we're introduced to someone socially, we usually dispense with the Mr. and Mrs., or, in a business situation, we get to first names rather quickly, provided the other is our equal. One exception is our doctor. We rarely get past the Dr. So-and-so barrier even after years of being a patient. But very quickly, usually at the first visit, the doctor gets to our first name. Lines of status are drawn. *I am the doctor. You are the patient. I am your superior.*

However, if the patient is a famous personality, a political figure, an industrial leader, the doctor will fall back on the honorific and it becomes Dr. and Mrs. Or the patient may take the offensive and call the doctor by his first name. I've seen a thirty-year-old doctor call a fifty-year-old patient Sally, while she called him Dr. Johnson. Then I've heard the same doctor call another patient, a young, well-known actor, Mr. Saville.

The title carries the metamessage of superiority and perhaps it helps the doctor-patient relationship, but, if so, why the exceptions? It seems more likely that what's at work is a matter of status.

In a boss-worker relationship the same status game holds true. It takes a long time before a worker can call the boss by his first name, but the boss may use the worker's first name from the first day on the job. An executive and his secretary follow the same rules, and so do a tenant and doorman or elevator operator, and of course with men and women on the job the same status rules hold with men having the upper edge. It works on all levels right down the line.

A friend of ours was faced with this status-name game recently in terms of her new domestic worker. When the woman came to work, she told our friend her name was Glenda Doyle.

"The ball was in our corner," my friend told me ruefully. "We could call her Glenda or Miss Doyle. We have two young children, and I wanted them to grow up respecting older people, no matter what their position. I decided they should call her Miss Doyle, and why shouldn't I too? She was certainly my equal in her field. I started off with Miss Doyle and the whole family accepted it.

"In time, since our relationship worked out so well, we became quite friendly, and when the time came for a raise I gave it to her and asked, 'Is everything all right?'

"She hesitated, then said 'Yes' reluctantly. 'I like the job, I really do. You and the kids . . . but there is one thing.'

" 'Yes?' I asked.

" 'I wish you'd all call me Glenda. Miss Doyle sounds so . . . well, cold and distant.'

"So much for respect!"

Our friend's experience plays up the dilemma of the metamessage behind a name or title. The formal title delivers a different metasignal in different circumstances and with different people. The domestic worker who is resentful of her role and feels the family has no respect for her will get a comforting message from the

Miss or Mrs., while the worker who feels part of the family will get a completely different one, a sense of exclusion.

When the domestic worker is black, a frequent title is *girl*. "My girl didn't come last Friday." It makes little difference if the *girl* is a grandmother. The metasignals around the name spell out a message. *You are inferior*. Blacks are acutely aware of this metamessage, and black men of any age have had to fight the use of *boy* for years, just as they had to fight for the right to be called mister. The name game is always one of status.

Try playing against the game. Call your elevator man Sir. Call your doctor by his first name. In either case the reaction can be upsetting. There are rules, but you cannot always go by them. You must be sensitive to the situation, to the other person's feelings, to elements of race, class, and profession. There will be times, in terms of your own self-respect, when you want to go against the accepted way of things.

Breaking the status rule in metacommunication is similar to asserting yourself. Using mister, doctor, sir are all methods of declaring *You are above me*. The first-name basis becomes an equalizer. The catch is, do you dare use it as an equal? Can you take the risk?

Do you dare use a first name to your boss?

To your girl friend's father?

To the cab driver whose name is on his license?

To the waiter in the restaurant?

6

Crossed Wires

THE TROUBLING CONTRADICTION

When two people talk, they communicate not only the meaning of the words they use but also their own feelings, attitudes, and intentions toward those words. As an example, an executive tells his boss about an important meeting he just had. "I met the client and we had a few drinks together and then we talked over the entire deal. The two of us got along very well. . . . I think we have a deal there."

There are two messages here. One is the objective reality of what he is saying. This lies in the meaning of his words. But there is another message he is trying to get across to his boss. *I am capable and friendly, an asset to the firm because people like me*. If his verbal message is delivered correctly, the hidden metamessage around it will come across too.

The boss may not be consciously aware that this man's voice is assured, confident, and enthusiastic, but all these qualities will have an impact on him at some hidden level.

If the same executive were to deliver the same message to his boss in a low, hesitant voice, the boss would doubt the words and wonder if he had any real deal with the client. No matter how aggressively certain the sense of a spoken message is, uncertain and self-doubting metasignals can contradict the message or confuse it.

This contradiction between the metamessage and the words is referred to as incongruence by Dr. Carl R. Rogers. Dr. Rogers, who has written extensively on communication, has developed the psychological concept of congruence, the matching of a person's experience with his awareness. If we carry this concept into the field of metacommunication, it becomes the matching of a person's words with his metasignals.

The woman who sighs deeply as she tells her husband that she's happy presents an incongruent picture. But which of the two statements is the truth, the despairing sigh or the words "I'm happy"?

Of the two, the metasignal is usually unconscious. We can lie quite easily with our words, but it is far more difficult to lie with the metasignals around the words. No matter how much enthusiasm we put into our voice when we say everything is going well, there will always be some betraying note to give us away. The metasignal is the more honest of the two simply because it's automatic and therefore unconscious.

The mother, admiring her little daughter's drawing, says, "What a wonderful picture!" But behind the admiration of the words is a flatness in how they're said. The true meaning of her remark becomes *Another scribble that I have to praise!*

The child, skilled in reading metacommunication, recognizes the truth behind the praise and, taking another look at her drawing, crumples it up in disgust and throws it away.

"I don't understand the child," her mother says, shaking her head. "I told her I liked the drawing." What she doesn't seem to realize is that her way of praising her daughter said just the opposite.

Adults tend to think that children can be deceived very easily by using the proper words and ignoring the metasignals. But children, logically enough, are more keenly attuned to the metasignals in our words than to the meaning of the words themselves. We tell our children to do one thing: "Come home on time." "Stay in the house." "Don't watch television." But all the while our metasignals say, *I don't really care what you do*. The child disobeys, secure in the knowledge that he won't be punished. He has picked up the real message behind our words.

When the child receives a hesitant metamessage and recognizes the uncertainty in his mother's voice, he knows that no matter what he's being told, Mother is unsure of what she means. No matter what he does, then, he's taking a chance. Guessing. The uncertainty is bound to upset him.

It is even more upsetting when a parent, or for that matter any adult, comes out with reassuring words in an emotional situation but uses the metasignals of fear, guilt, or even hatred.

Mother may say, "I'm not really mad at Daddy. We're just having a disagreement." But the child has picked up the furious, barely controlled tone in his mother's voice. He hears the low, intense pitch and knows what it means.

Such messages confuse children and frighten them. Often, in self-defense, they will learn how to manipulate their parents in order to protect themselves. Some will become naughty in order to shift attention away from the parent under attack. Others may try to be overly good to prevent their parents' anger.

Why are children so sensitive to metacommunication? We can understand the reason when we consider that children learn metacommunication before they learn to talk. We coo at our babies and make all sorts of loving noises that mean nothing in words but everything in metasignals. Our noises tell the baby that he's loved, secure, adored without ever having to use words.

For all that time before they learn to speak, children must rely only on the metasignals we send them. Is it any wonder that once they learn to speak they carry a better understanding of those signals than they do of words? Metacommunication is an emotional language, a language of feeling, and it is learned by a child when his emotions are still ahead of his intellect.

That early recognition that metasignals are more important than words stays with us all our lives. In adulthood, a woman may hear her lover say, "I love you," but sense a doubt behind his words, a questioning metamessage that even he is not fully aware of, and she pulls away, unsatisfied and unhappy. The old saying proves true. "It's not what you say, it's the way that you say it."

The way that we say things must match what we are saying if we are to communicate accurately. The metamessage must fit the words. We must be congruent.

THE INCONGRUENT MAN

Dr. Rogers' concept of congruence speaks of matching a person's awareness with his experience, or, put differently, a congruent man is one who is in touch with his own feelings. Paradoxically, it becomes easier to understand congruence when we consider incongruence.

Martin is an incongruent man. In his business dealings, he confuses his associates and puzzles his clients. At a recent sales conference, speaking on a relatively unimportant issue, Martin's voice was raised and his face was furious. Feeling that the point in question was deeply important to him, the rest of his associates gave in and the meeting continued. Afterward, one of his close friends on the board drew him aside.

"I didn't know you felt so deeply about that sales territory."

Surprised, Martin said, "What do you mean, deeply? I'd like to see it split up, and I'm glad we decided to, but it's no big deal."

Puzzled, his friend protested, "But you spoke so vehemently about it. You were so angry."

"Me angry?" Martin shook his head. "You must be kidding. I wasn't angry at all. I was just presenting my ideas."

Frowning, his friend dropped the subject, but from that point on he no longer trusted Martin. "The thing is," he confided to another member of the board, "I think he's two-faced."

But Martin was a completely honest man. What his friend didn't realize was the fact that Martin had no concept of his own very inappropriate behavior. He had been sending out very strong metasignals of anger and deep involvement, but he hadn't been feeling any of those signals. The imbalance between what he felt and what he appeared to feel was so great that it confused everyone who listened to him.

Anger is not the only incongruous signal we send out. Some of us signal deep depression with flat tones and expressionless voices when we are not at all depressed. Others may signal a bright, happy feeling when they are miserable. In the beginning of President Carter's term, his physical signals seemed very confusing. He would make a devastating remark and accompany it with a smile. The smile had no relationship to the words, and, like an incongruous verbal signal, it threw us all off. Just what did he mean with it? Was he smiling ironically at the terrible thing he had said? Sarcastically? Sympathetically? Or was the smile just a nervous tic?

A smile is a body-language signal, but a laugh is a verbal metasignal, and many people use it incongruously, laughing a bit nervously when they come out with a very serious statement. The laugh becomes an apology, a nervous reaction to what they are saying, but the effect on anyone who hears the misplaced signal is one of confusion—of incongruence.

The President's smile has been cleaned up. In his position, he can afford to have a department concerned with the Presidential image, with the clothes he wears, the speech he uses, and the gestures he makes. Congruence, which signals strength and assurance, is always an important end result of any attempt at image shaping. That's why, with each public appearance, the President becomes more congruent. There is an important lesson here. Congruence can be learned. No matter how mismatched our words and metasignals are, we can sort them out, bring them from the unconscious to the conscious level, and then make sure that they fit each other.

Martin, the businessman, had he been open to improving himself, might have listened more carefully to his friend's complaint. Instead of protesting, "I wasn't angry," he might have answered, "I wasn't angry, but I must have sounded angry. What did I do to give that impression?"

If he had had the insight to go that far, he would have been on his way to an understanding of his problem and to an eventual matching of his metacommunication with his speech.

Sandra, an attractive and open young woman, is another example of an incongruent person. "I'm a very social person," she confesses. "I like people, but I just don't seem able to hold onto friends. I'll meet someone at a party or at work and I'll think we've really hit it off, but then, when I suggest we get together again, they always have an excuse. Like this one woman at work—I've called her twice now to invite her over for dinner. She's my age and single and I know we have a lot in common, but she brushed me off very fast. I got the message. She wasn't interested in becoming my friend."

As Sandra tells her story it becomes clear that her words do not match her manner. The intensity in her voice, the passionate melody of her speech, the way she emphasizes the wrong words—all of her metacues are too strong for what she is saying. She speaks in an overwhelming way and she frightens off the people she tries to befriend.

"I would like to know you better," she says, but the way she says it communicates a much stronger message. *I want to know all about you. I want to tell you all about me. I want to be more than a friend, much, much more!*

Most of the time her metasignals are not in tune with the situation nor with her own expectations. She is an emotional runaway who comes on too fast and too strong.

The first step any incongruent person, any Sandra or Martin, must take to achieve congruence is toward objectivity. If you suspect that you are incongruent, you must step back and look at yourself or, more important, listen to yourself. In many cases you can do this through the eyes and ears of a friend. Get someone you know and trust to talk to you frankly. Find out just how he sees you and hears you, and listen to what he says without fighting it. Once you can become aware of the incongruence, you can work to correct it.

When a friend fails, a tape recorder can be a useful tool in discovering incongruity. Playing it back can give you an objective clue to your mismatching and something to stack your new performance against. It can become a record of your progress toward congruence.

THE GASLIGHT GAME

There is a danger in relying on someone else to discover whether or not you are congruent. All too often you will run into someone who will try to attach their own metasignals to something you have said. This is a very common situation within a family. Fred brings Alice home to dinner, and afterward he asks his mother how she liked her.

"She seems like a nice girl," Mother says thoughtfully.

But Fred chooses to read something else into her statement. "You sound as if you don't approve."

Now at this point Mother neither approves nor disapproves. In all fairness she doesn't know the girl well enough to judge. But Fred has his own doubts about Alice. He's really not sure he wants to date her again, and he would like to use his mother's judgment to get off the hook. He wants to hear, in her nonjudgmental statement, his own doubts—and indeed, those doubts are so strong that he does manage to hear them, or to convince himself that he does.

His mother, seeing that Fred has come to a decision about Alice, says tentatively, "Perhaps she isn't the right girl for you?"

In turn, finally getting the feedback he's fishing for, Fred defuses his own guilt by attacking his mother's judgment. "You never like any of the girls I bring home!"

"Now that's just not true . . ." and a family argument is off and running. What Fred has managed is a form of scapegoating. By reading a nonexistent metasignal of disapproval into his mother's voice, he has been able to make a decision without taking the blame for it. A fast mental shuffle has convinced him of his mother's incongruity on the subject of Alice.

It's a handy way of lessening his own feelings of guilt, and in truth no harm is done by it unless his mother is conned into believing that she initiated Fred's break with Alice. "Did I really sound that disapproving?" she may ask herself later, and be troubled by the possibility that she can't control her own inner emotions—even when she's not aware of them.

This self-doubt, if the procedure happens often enough, can turn into a subtle form of gaslighting (a phrase from the Hitchcock thriller *Gaslight*, in which the husband convinces his wife that she's going mad).

Gaslighting can be done unconsciously when it occurs between two people and one constantly puts his own anxiety on the other. If the other allows herself to fall into the role, she will eventually come to believe that *she* is the anxious one, the upset one, the nervous one, and, in extreme cases, the crazy one.

Karla and Ian play this game over their son. Ian will start it with, "Billy's not home yet."

"I wonder where he is?" Karla asks. "Basketball practice is over by now, usually. . . ."

"You're upset over the kid," Ian decides.

"No . . . I just thought he should be back by now."

But Ian interrupts. "You always get yourself into a stew about him. You're too anxious."

"Well, I do worry sometimes. . . ."

"Worry? My God, you're a walking case of mother hysteria if the kid's even a few minutes late. What time is he due home, anyway?"

Karla ends up the guilty one here, but Ian is really the one who started the worrying. Their metacommunication gives us the clue. When Karla first wonders where her son is, her voice is thoughtful and pitched low. She is honestly trying to figure out what detained him, but without anxiety. Ian's accusation, "You're upset over the kid," is loud and anxiety-provoking.

Karla picks this up, but knows she isn't worried. She tries to explain but ends up by doubting her own feelings. She figures that she must be anxious because Ian has told her, often enough, that she's an anxious mother.

Ian and Karla have played this gaslight game for a long time, and bit by bit Karla has accepted the role Ian gave her, the anxious, near-hysterical wife and mother. Perhaps she even likes the role in some perverse way. If she didn't she could have aborted the entire game in the beginning by telling Ian, "No. I am not upset. I may be concerned, but that doesn't make me an anxious or hysterical mother."

In standing up for herself this way, Karla would be taking an initial step toward congruence. The lesson is to be sure you don't hear a nonexistent metasignal in your own voice, a signal someone else claims to hear. It is too easy to believe that you wanted to say a thing, deep down, because someone else *heard* it in your voice.

The other side of this incongruent coin is the trick of overwhelming someone else with your own metasignals. The mother who tells her child, "You'll really love these vegetables," is trying to do just this. So is the woman who asks her lover, "You really love me, don't you?" and so is the eager young man who tells his girl friend, "This is absolutely the best restaurant you've ever been to."

The way the other should feel is spelled out in advance. The other person is overwhelmed by the intensity of the metacommunication. Oddly enough, such metasignals which project your own feelings onto someone else are always stronger than usual. The excitement, interest, and passion of such projections must be exceptionally strong in order to convince the other person.

It becomes very hard, if you are a partner in such an exchange, to stand up for your own feelings and say, "No. I didn't like the food," or, "I don't really love you," or, "The restaurant was second rate."

Someone else has forced an incongruent attitude on you, and as water seeks its own level, so human emotions tend toward congruence. If we are well balanced and someone puts us into an incongruent position, we struggle to get out of it.

It is easier to achieve congruence by accepting the other's emotion, by agreeing to like the food, the restaurant, or even the lover. It is much harder to reject the emotion and find congruence by insisting on the truth of how you feel. The child pushed toward loving the vegetables has the easiest time of it. He can resist his mother's overwhelming push and say, "I hate spinach!" It's expected of him because we all accept the fact that children have strong food preferences.

The adult lover has a much harder time. Another person's psyche is involved in his rejection. Only a heel will hurt a woman who asks for love. The young lady who questions the restaurant her boyfriend is touting shows a certain ingratitude as well as social awkwardness.

EMOTIONAL BLACKMAIL

In all of these attempts to put your own emotions onto someone else there is a touch of emotional blackmail. I once had a friend with a severe mother problem who told me of a visit home when he was a grown man. "For dessert, Mother baked a chocolate cake and a sponge cake, and asked me which I wanted. I said the chocolate cake, and she looked at me in dismay. 'What's wrong? Don't you like my sponge cake?' "

Here the emotion is guilt, laid on with a classic double bind. He must make a choice, but any choice carries the metasignal of rejection. "I finally learned," he told me, "to choose a piece of each."

The person who develops a skill in putting these uncomfortable metasignals onto others usually develops the additional skill of enlisting other people to strengthen the situation. In school, a teacher will listen to Jimmy's answer, and then enlist the class with, "We all know Jimmy is wrong, don't we, class?" This is a classic example, but it's on an adult-child level. The enlisting of others is just as common between adults, especially in certain marriages where it becomes a form of emotional blackmail.

The wife or husband will save up criticisms for an evening spent with close friends, and enlist the friends to put down the mate. "John wants to trade in the Chevy instead of selling it privately. What do you think of that?" A simple statement and a question, but delivered with all the sarcastic impact that John's wife can muster. Her voice tells her friends that John is too lazy to sell the car privately and too stupid to realize he will lose money by trading it in.

Or another example. "Rita asked her mother to come for a month's visit," Rita's husband announces to their dinner guests. The verbal message is a statement of a fact, but it is delivered in a voice of complete amazement and disbelief. Rita's sanity is being scrutinized. How could anyone in her right mind want Rita's mother to stay for a month? He hasn't said it outright, but the guests have been involved in this kind of undercover blackmail before, and they know exactly what he means.

Then there is the mother-in-law who enlists her daughter's husband by saying, "Do you really like Nel's hair that way?" The accent she uses on *that*, the pitch of her voice, the disdainful tone mixed with respect say clearly, *My daughter doesn't realize how unbecoming her hair is, but you and I are smart enough to know she should never wear it like that*. In this case, it says even more. It tells the son-in-law that mother is very critical of his wife and she would like him to join her, to be in league with her when she opens her veiled attack.

In a situation like this it takes a strong person to be aware of what's happening, to understand the strong emotional overtones in the metacommunication and then stand back and say, "I won't become involved. Don't tell me what I feel."

But in every case this is exactly what must be done

if you are to handle such enlistments. The metamessages handed out match the irony, sarcasm, or criticism of the enlister. To keep from being an enlistee, you must prevent these emotions from being confused with your own.

If you don't, if you accept the proffered enlistment, you will automatically seek to balance out the incongruity and match what you say to what you are supposed to feel. You will strive for congruence even if it means accepting someone else's evaluation in preference to your own.

A WOMAN'S INTUITION

The difficulty an incongruent person faces in our highly communicative society is matched by the difficulty of those who must live with him or work with him. They are constantly thrown into confusion by the mismatched signals he sends out. One solution, unkind as it is, is to avoid him. Another is to try to cut through the confusion.

A wife of an incongruent man will often develop a nonlistening technique to handle him. She may avoid the metasignals entirely and focus in on the meaning of the words, or, if the metasignals are more honest, she will ignore the words and listen only to the metamessages. This technique may be labeled intuition, but it is often the only way of coping with incongruence. The wife gains a reputation for understanding her husband, but the danger is that often the understanding becomes ignoring. "Don't pay any attention to Harry's blustering. He doesn't mean it."

The husband, in turn, is given a go-ahead to continue his incongruence, and he may even gain a certain satisfaction out of it. But he becomes more and more difficult to live with and less and less tolerated.

We've chosen the husband as the incongruent one in this marriage because it usually happens that way. A wife can be incongruous, of course. We're all familiar with the "Gracie Allen Syndrome," when the words and the metasignals are completely mismatched. But this behavior is rarely encouraged. It's not considered cute or attractive in a grown woman and most wives learn to shape up.

The husband's incongruence is easier to get away with. The autocratic father is still approved of, and incongruence can be confused with autocracy. It may even boost the husband's ego, and the wife goes along with it because there is a manipulative effect. If she is the only one who can understand him, she is essential.

When the congruent partner in a marriage adapts like this, the adaptation is usually a strain and many problems arise. On a very simple level, let's take an intimate moment when the husband says, "Yes. I love you." The words are right, but his tone is flat and dispirited.

Should she accept his statement at face value and reply with her own declaration of love? Should she make some physical overture, or should she pay attention to the flatness of his statement, the lack of real melody in his voice, the slight rise in pitch at the end that we associate with a question, not a statement?

The pause to sort out all of this, to search for the proper answer can, in itself, be interpreted as metacommunication. "If you take so long to answer, can you really care about me?"

Such incongruence, when it gets to a personal level, may be more than the most intuitive wife can manage. She is always faced with the danger of misinterpretation in an area too important to make a mistake in. Does "Yes, I love you" mean what it says, or "I don't but I won't hurt your feelings" or "I need love so desperately I'll even take yours" or "I can't love anyone" or what?

After many years with an incongruent partner she may be able to sort out the answers, interpret the flat tone, and do it instantly—to dredge up that old "intuition."

She might answer his "Yes. I love you" with "I'm sorry, dear. Did you have a rough day?" and see nothing strange about her answer. She has simply interpreted his metacommunication as *I feel bad, tired and upset,* and she's given an appropriate answer to his statement of love.

Not every wife, even after living with her husband for years, can cut through the incongruent messages to get at the heart of the matter. She may have given up long ago and simply turns off when she gets an incongruent message. But it's more common for the partner to see through the incongruence to get at the heart of the message.

It is usually in sexual areas that the greatest incongruities occur, perhaps because so many of us have been taught that sex is not a proper subject for clear discussion. The wife who wishes sex will rarely approach it directly. If she voices her interest, it's usually in the metasignals, not in the words, and it's often done by pushing the wish onto the husband. "I can tell you want sex tonight" or "If you want sex, okay. . . ." Sometimes the spoken message is less direct. "You look very handsome tonight!" or "We're finally alone!"

Most husbands pick up the metacommunication at once, and all goes well. But occasionally there will be a stubborn "But do *you* want sex?" and unless the wife answers firmly, it can lead to the profitless "No, but I thought you did" or "I don't really care, one way or another" or "I just thought we ought to. It's been so long. . . ."

The inevitable end of this conversation becomes, "Well! If that's all it means to you . . ." and leads to frustration.

The point is, for any communication to work, very close attention must be paid to the metasignals as well as the words. If they are incongruent, and you know the sender, you must choose the correct statement on the basis of that knowledge. If you don't know the sender, you'll just have to take a chance.

THE OBLIQUE MESSAGE

Unfortunately, congruence is often difficult to achieve. Our unconscious seems to take over, and no matter how smoothly we lie with our words, a subtle metasignal destroys it all. One of the ways many of us use to avoid this is an oblique approach. We talk about something else instead of this thing that really concerns us, and we allow all our stored-up anger and frustration or unhappiness to pour over into that oblique statement.

Take the case of Mary and Peter. Twenty-two years old, Mary has just moved in with her boyfriend, Peter. It is the first time she has ever *lived with a man* and she is a little scared about it and uncertain—but both of them want it to work out.

"We'll share everything," Peter tells her confidently. "The food, the cleaning up—it's bound to be cheaper than two apartments."

But after a week or so, Mary realizes that Peter is

not doing his share of the cleaning up, and her own load is doubled. She cares about Peter and wants their relationship to be honest, but because of her own vulnerability she is unable to speak out honestly. Instead she keeps all her feelings hidden until one night, after dinner, tired and angry, she strikes out in an oblique way.

"This apartment is just too small for all this clutter." She's sitting across from Peter at the table, but she's looking at the wall as she speaks.

Peter senses the annoyance in her voice, but he isn't quite sure of what she's annoyed about, or even if she's addressing him. Does Mary mean that she doesn't want to live with him anymore? Is she having second thoughts about their relationship? Maybe she thinks they should get a bigger place—or is she really saying he's a bit of a slob? The last thought makes him uneasy and guilty. Jokingly, he says, "The room does have a lived-in look. . . ."

Mary swallows, and in a low voice murmurs, "You don't love me."

"Love you?" Bewildered, Peter stares at her. "What in hell are you talking about? Why are you so upset?"

"I'm not upset," Mary answers in a tight, controlled voice.

"You sure could have fooled me. Come on, what's the matter?"

Mary is a woman who has never learned true congruence. She always used metacommunication in an oblique way. She learned the trick as a child, from her mother. Her mother never made an outright statement about her feelings. She would tell her husband, "That dripping faucet in the bathroom is driving me crazy!" when she wanted to say, *We need a new bathroom sink*. Or "Joan Lockward told me her husband got a big raise. Isn't he in your department?" When she really meant *Why can't you bring home enough money to give me the things I want?* Or "The dog's made a mess on the rug again today" instead of *I never wanted a dog in the house.*

As a child, Mary was confused at first by her mother's oblique messages, but she soon cam not only to live with them but also to adapt them to her own use. She learned never to come right out with what was bothering her or with what she really felt. She had decided that this was the proper way for women to relate to men.

Under Peter's prodding, Mary finally opened up and told him exactly what was troubling her, that she had been doing his share of the work as well as her own.

"But why didn't you tell me straight out?" he insisted. "Look, living together isn't a guessing game. I hear anger in your voice and how do I know what's wrong? You tell me the apartment is too small, and I might be out looking for a bigger one. How would that solve the problem? From now on you level with me."

"I'll try," Mary promised.

When the problem is exposed, as Peter forced it to be, it can often be solved. But if the oblique messages continue, there can never be a solution because nobody can zero in on the problem. There is always a substitute problem in the way thrown up as a camouflage.

There are families where both the oblique approach and an incongruity interfere with any true communication, and there is a malfunctioning in almost any discussion.

The Green family is a perfect example. They are unhappy people locked into adversary roles and never quite understanding how they tear each other down.

On a typical evening, when Father Green comes

home from work, Mother Green says in an accusing voice, "You never talk to me. You just walk in that door and all you ask is when is dinner." Her words match her angry metasignals.

In a tired and uninterested tone, Father Green says, "What's to say? Nothing happened today." Then, recalling his day at work, he decides to share some of it. His voice picks up a metasignal of interest and he adds, "The boss was mad as hell because the duplicator . . ."

Mother Green interrupts before he can get the story underway. She keeps on the same subject, his boss, but her concern is somewhere else. "Your boss thinks he's God. He ought to give you some credit for the way you work. You've been there longer than anyone, and yet you let him walk all over you."

An oblique situation is coming on. Father's concern for the anecdote he has been telling has been instantly dried up by his wife's anger, apparently directed at the boss, but in reality directed at him. Father Green switches back to the same uninterested tone he started with, his metamessage to turn off or turn away her anger. "I can't get into a hassle with him about . . ."

Now the argument has been brought to her ground, and Mother Green wades in, matching her words to the contempt in her underlying metasignals. Her interrupting him before he can finish a sentence is another metasignal that says, *I'm not really concerned with you as a person—or with your feelings. I'm concerned with telling you what's wrong.*

"I can read you like a book," she goes on. "The big silent one. Always taking all the crap that's handed out to you."

Resigned and apologetic, he tries to defuse her anger. "You're probably right. I just don't like to argue over . . ."

But she won't accept his peace offering. She interrupts again. "If you'd just learn to open your mouth. You've got to tell people off or they'll walk all over you. You're so damned quiet—you don't even talk to me. What kind of life do you think it is for me?" Now her metacommunication changes from anger to self-pity.

There is no villain in this piece. Even while she's complaining, Mother Green feels a sick sensation in the pit of her stomach. "My God," she tells herself in a blinding flash of insight, "I sound just like my mother-in-law, always yelling, interrupting, hysterical! But he drives me to it!"

In a way she's right. Father Green has picked her just because she resembles his own mother, with the same angry, controlling, critical personality. He feels safer, without being aware of it, when he is treated like a child. So, while hating it all on a conscious level, unconsciously his metasignals all encourage his wife's behavior. He seldom starts a conversation, but his silences speak louder than words, and they are often used for manipulation. He's not available for comment, or for discipline, or for loving or accepting. He's present physically, but his metasignals, voiced or silent, indicate that he's not interested.

At the dinner table, the Greens' teenage son may ask his father a question. Father Green hesitates, clears his throat, and begins tentatively, "Well, I'm not completely sure . . ."

His hesitation and his choice of words have signaled his distaste at being drawn into any problem. Mother Green, interpreting these signals, rushes in to answer the question herself. The son, even though he's been through this routine a number of times, feels he must challenge his mother. His question was asked less for an answer than for a commitment on the part of his father. He's growing into manhood, and he has a desperate need for his father to show some strength. Resenting his father's hesitation as much as his mother's interruptions, he says, "Just once, let Dad speak for himself!"

There is a metamessage of anger here, and underlying it a plea. Mother defuses both with a hurt tone. "Is it my fault he won't speak up? How do you think I feel when he sits there like a lump?"

The son hesitates, the anger gone but the plea still alive. "You never give him a chance."

Seeing her way to victory, Mother Green appeals to her husband. "Is that true? Tell the child. Haven't I pleaded with you to talk? Is everything my fault?" Then, including them both, "Do you think it's easy when you both gang up on me?"

The son's plea gives way to despair and guilt, and he looks down, avoiding her eyes as he murmurs, "I'm sorry. I guess I'm out of line," and in his voice we hear the echo of Father Green's metasignals, the same malfunctioning communication. He has learned the danger of speaking out truthfully, and he realizes, now, the value of his father's silence as a weapon.

The mother has won this round, but there are no real winners in this conflict. Inside she realizes that she has lost, that a family interaction should not be turned into a struggle for dominance.

THE MAN IN CHARGE

In the Green family, the mother held the reins of power. In the Brown family, the father was definitely the man in charge, not only of the family but also of himself. Mr. Brown achieved his dominance by never allowing himself to express any metasignals of weakness, and yet this too was a technique that could backfire. Mr. Brown used the "I'm fine. I can handle it" routine. This message is one that never varies, and the person who sends it is never able to admit he is not fine or unable to handle things. He must always be in control.

Most of us stay in control of the everyday problems of life, but there are often times when we must turn to others for support or help. Few of us are ashamed to say, "I had a lousy day," or "I feel awful!" or "Can you give me a hand with this. I can't manage it alone."

The man, like Mr. Brown, who never does this must always present a competent personality to the world although he may, in truth, be a very frightened person. He knows he must keep himself in rigid control and he carries this control over to his metacommunication.

"Livia, I'll be home a little late tonight," Mr. Brown tells his wife from a pay phone on a highway. His voice is slow, the words measured, the tone slightly harsh, and there is a flatness to his speech.

His wife senses something is not quite right, but she is never able to pick up his exact metacues. She asks, "Problems at the office?"

Her husband's voice gains strength, but is still tightly controlled. "I've had an accident."

Frightened, his wife asks, "Are you hurt? Should I come?"

"I'm fine. I have everything under control. I'll get a lift after the tow truck takes the car to the garage."

There is a pause as Livia assimilates the message. Of course her husband's all right. He's always all right. Nothing ever upsets him. "I'll keep your dinner warm in the oven."

But after he hangs up, Mr. Brown slumps in the phone booth, his head pounding, his body trembling. He is not all right. He is scared to death. He had a close brush with death and it's sheer luck he walked away from it. What he needs, desperately, is the comfort of another person, his wife's sympathy and understanding, and it is just this he cannot ask for.

Later that night, over a warmed-up dinner, he becomes more and more upset until he turns on his wife angrily when she asks how the car is. "All you're interested in is the damned car!"

In bewilderment she says, "But you insisted you were all right."

"I handled it," he tells her stiffly, closing down that instant of revelation. "Did you expect I'd fall apart over the car flipping over?"

"Well, I would have been terrified."

"Well, I'm not you. There isn't much I can't handle." But there is less self-satisfaction in his tone than critical reproval. Why didn't she comfort him? Reassure him? Slowly his wife is becoming aware of what really happened, but his metasignals are still too confusing to cue her in properly. The only thing she can do now is to try and shrug it off. Her husband is like that, always hiding things.

If, in truth, Mr. Brown were content to hide this, it would all blow over. But the fact is that he doesn't want it hidden. He wants his own cool-headedness praised. He wants sympathy and understanding, but he hasn't allowed his need for it to show. His own desire to dominate the situation has kept him from revealing the complete truth.

Mr. Brown's incongruence is impossible for his wife to cut through, for it only shows itself in times of crisis. But these are just the times when Mr. Brown needs the help and sympathy he refuses to ask for.

7

Coded Transmissions

THE SEMANTICS GAME

We all play the Semantics Game to one degree or another. The game is simple; its rules are easily learned—and its effect can be devastating. The object of the game is to define a quality, a place, a person, an object, with words whose metasignals are so loaded that they contradict the meaning of your statement. You can play the Semantics Game positively or negatively. A negative game is usually destructive, and if it's played with finesse, you can assault someone and if challenged answer with "But I only said what was obvious" or "I was just being honest" or, best of all, "You're reading things into my remarks."

Take Chris. At thirty he is married and into a good career in advertising art. Chris is a master of the destructive Semantics Game. When he was courting his wife, Lois, he enthusiastically described her younger brother, Jim, as "very outspoken, just like your father."

The admiration in his voice pleased Lois. She was close to her brother, though he had always overshadowed her. She valued her boyfriend's opinion, and she felt that his description of her brother and father was complimentary and accurate. They were both outspoken, a word that suggested honest and forthright too.

Now, a few years after their marriage, Chris is not so eager to please her. In fact, there is more tension than love in their relationship. Lois's brother came to supper the other night, and after he left Chris said in a despairing voice, "You know, Jim is just as loud as ever."

Lois was crushed. She had come to think of Jim as outspoken. Was Chris right? Was he just loud? The word *loud* sounded harsh and unflattering to her ears, and the metasignal behind it made her feel a little ashamed of her brother.

Chris, with that one word, had planted a doubt in his wife's estimation of her brother, and indirectly of her father too. But Chris is so good at negative messages that in the last few years he has gradually undermined Lois's feelings about her brother and herself as well.

Suppose that Lois had challenged him on the word *loud*. "I thought Jim was outspoken."

Chris would have come up with a confusing answer. "Listen, you know I like the guy. Sure he's outspoken, too outspoken. In my book that's loud."

By adding *too* to *outspoken* Chris has changed the entire concept of the word. Outspoken is now equated with loud.

Chris carries this destructive Semantics Game over

into his job. He will look at a colleague's work and find, with unerring precision, the one word to deflate the artist. "The layout's all right, but the color's too raw."

Now the important gambit in the game is the use of a word that describes something accurately but contains a destructive metasignal. Chris could have said, "The color's too strong." Both *raw* and *strong* describe the color, but raw has a negative metasignal. Strong has a positive one.

Chris, with his built-in destructive streak, carries the Semantics Game into every part of his life. In a restaurant, over a business lunch, he'll say the food is "very well done." Not good, or tasty, or cooked well, but *well done*. The message is clear. The food is overcooked and not too tasty. He waits until his host orders a wine, tastes it, and delivers his judgment with one word. "Adequate." The dessert, he decides, is "very . . . [pause] sweet." The use of *very* and the pause add enough to sweet to make it undesirable.

There is no area that Chris can't invade with his Semantics Game. Even the new secretary the firm has hired, an attractive young woman with a very delicate complexion, is characterized as "colorless" by Chris. The department head, an economical man trying to work within the department's budget, is seen by Chris as "cheap"—and so it goes.

The point of each put-down, of course, is somehow to bolster Chris's ego. If everyone else is wrong, then he must have an edge on rightness. What often happens, however, in such a situation, is that Chris is gradually seen as the kind of person nobody is comfortable with. His friends begin to avoid him, and when an opportunity for advancement comes, Chris is considered "just too—well, too negative." His assistant is promoted over his head, and this has its desired effect. To save face, he quits, and his office breathes a sigh of relief.

His wife, Lois, can't solve the problem that easily. She is unaware of his game playing, but each put-down is eroding their relationship a little more. She can't fight it because she doesn't understand what's happening. The fault, she feels, lies in herself, and she tries desperately to improve an impossible situation.

When Lois, unable to cope with Chris, has what her doctor refers to as a mild breakdown, he suggests she try some therapy with Dr. Gordon, a clinical psychologist. In her first session, Lois, describing her symptoms, tells Dr. Gordon that she's very depressed and withdrawn. Chris has told her so.

Dr. Gordon is a game player too, but he plays the positive Semantics Game. "I wouldn't call it depressed," he tells her thoughtfully. "I'd say you're disheartened and probably you're a quiet person, not withdrawn."

That struck a chord in Lois and she told Dr. Gordon about her brother Jim. "Jim's the . . ." She started to say loud one, and then remembered Chris's early description of Jim. "Jim's the outspoken one in the family. Like my dad. I guess I took a backseat to both."

Dr. Gordon nodded, and later when she characterized Jim as aggressive, he stopped her. "You could say he's sure of himself, too, couldn't you?"

Thinking it over, Lois agreed. Jim was that, and as the sessions went on, the gradual weaning from negative to positive went on too. Instead of *anxious*, Dr. Gordon saw her as *concerned*. Instead of *nervous*, he felt she was *stressed*. Their son, whom Chris characterized as *hyperactive*, Dr. Gordon suggested might be a *lively* boy.

"It's strange," Lois told him after a few months. "I'm able to handle so much more now. I've learned a great deal here, but you know, the strangest thing is that I've discovered that so much of what I worry about seems to melt away if I turn that semantic corner and look at it just a little bit differently—or use a different word to describe it."

Lois learned something else too. She learned not to be a passive participant in her husband's destructive behavior. She began to challenge him when he delivered his put-downs and then used his innocent disclaimers "I was just being honest" or "You can't deny what I said, can you?" Now Lois would answer, "That's an unkind way to describe me," or "That's a very destructive word you used."

All of us play the Semantics Game to some extent, and playing it is not always bad. There are times when we need negative words. We have to think of certain people as villains because they are villains, of certain things as bad because they are bad. But just as often we can make bad situations better by using a different word with a different connotation. Tact and sensitivity, when used with honesty, can make a negative game player into a positive one.

We must become aware that every word carries a trail of hidden meanings, metasignals, and messages. When Lois realized how much negative communication was going on in her marriage, she started really listening to her husband and then to her friends too. When one of them, Carolyn, came back from her vacation, Lois asked her and a few neighbors over for coffee.

Ruth, who lived across the street, started playing the negative version of the Semantics Game before her coat was off.

"Darling! You've lost so much weight," she purred at Carolyn. "You look positively skinny!"

Defensively, Carolyn said, "Well, not so much. I needed to drop a few pounds." Her answer was almost apologetic, yet she did look good. Thoughtfully, Lois began to consider Ruth's remark. There was enthusiasm in her *darling,* and Carolyn was caught off guard. She expected something positive after that, but the next words were delivered with destructive metasignals. The tone was unbelieving and the *positively* enhanced *skinny,* a word that signaled *old, unattractive, gaunt*.

Lois decided that a round of the positive Semantics Game was in order. When she was alone with Carolyn in the kitchen, she said, "You *have* lost weight. You look *sensationally* slim."

She delivered the same message as Ruth's, but her metamessage said, *You did it and I knew you could.* Her choice of slim (positive) as opposed to skinny (negative) or even thin (neutral), was very deliberate. It was also honest and sensitive to Carolyn's feelings.

The lesson we can learn from this exchange, the opposing of slim to skinny, is the importance of the culture around us. Seventy years ago thin and slim were as negative as skinny when applied to a woman. The metamessage was *unattractive,* even *sickly*. Today, with fashion's emphasis on slender women, slim has come into its own. Its metamessages are *stylish, chic, desirable*. Skinny, however, is still loaded with negative cues, *bony, emaciated, weak*.

Most words have neutral metasignals behind them, their total meaning contained in their definition. This is particularly true of adjectives. Strong, weak, happy, sad, beautiful, handsome usually mean just what they say. But some adjectives have very strong positive or negative connotations. A list of some will make this clear.

Try applying some of the words on the list to a person you've just met, a business associate or a friend. Pick a negative adjective and think of all its connotations. Then take the positive one and see if using it helps you see the person in a different light.

POSITIVE	NEGATIVE
Talkative	Gabby
Clever	Cunning
Subtle	Sly
Sensual	Loose
Humility	Servility
Perseverance	Stubbornness
Lonely	Forlorn
Compliment	Flattery
Simplicity	Plainness
Selective	Picky
Skeptical	Suspicious
Satisfied	Smug
Suave	Glib
Sensitive	Touchy

WHAT'S IN A NAME?

Very often the metasignals in a word depend on our own background and on the incidents that have made us, as individuals, aware of a special word. This is particularly true of names. One generation's popular name becomes another generation's lost one. Julius was popular in the early twenties, but it's almost a dead name now. Jennifer was unusual in the fifties, and now it's the most popular girl's name. Samuel and Max have died away, and anyone named Mark must be in his twenties. Brenda ran its popular course, and so did Barbara. Each, in its heyday, signaled something, but the signals change and fade away with time.

Recently, after the television show "Roots," many black children were named after the main characters, Kizzy and Kunta. The names were associated with intense emotions. A sense of history, background, and pride were metamessages behind them.

Hollywood, in its earlier years, was very sensitive to the nuances of names. It rechristened most of its stars and would-be stars with names that sent out metamessages of glamour and excitement, of good clean Americana or something provocatively foreign. Frances Gumm was changed to Judy Garland, Doris von Kappelhoff to Doris Day, the WASP girls next door. Archie Leach became Cary Grant, Sarah Jane Fulks metamorphosed into Jane Wyman. Emanuel Goldenberg ended up as Edward G. Robinson, Bernard Schwartz as Tony Curtis, and Virginia McMath as Ginger Rogers, Jules Garfinkle turned into Jules Garfield for the stage, but Hollywood considered even Jules touchy and made it John Garfield.

In many instances the "Jewishness" was taken out of a name, and sometimes the Italian. Anna Italiano was changed to Anne Bancroft, but in other cases just the homely sound of the name was changed: Gumm and Leach. The finished product always had to be euphonious, and the name had to signal solid WASP—Joan Crawford (Lucille Le Sueur), Rock Hudson (Roy Scherer); or the exotica of a Myrna Loy or Theda Bara; or the foreign sensuality of a Valentino or Rita Hayworth. In every case the name was a metasignal to arouse some deep emotion in the listener.

Today, many of our movie stars keep their ethnic names. Al Pacino, George Segal, Barbra Streisand,

Robert De Niro, Richard Dreyfuss all came to Hollywood after they had gained some stature on the stage. The theater has usually demanded talent first while Hollywood wanted the slick packaging of personality. But as America becomes more secure in its own image we are willing to accept ethnic names for actors and even politicians.

Twenty years ago it was unthinkable that a Kennedy would be President or a Kissinger Secretary of State.

Some names are hard to live with. Johnny Cash's funny song about a boy named Sue tells of the hardening process a man must go through when he has a girl's name. Any boy who grew up named Percy, Bruce, Marion, Marmaduke, or any other of the unusual first names parents sometimes choose knows of that hardening, just as girls who grew up with the unusual Blossom, Desiree, Exquisita know of the ridicule other children can put them through. Their names signal *unusual, not to be trusted, peculiar, funny.*

Often our feelings about a name are the results of knowing someone with that name. A friend told us that as a child he had a counselor in camp who treated him in a cruel and embarrassing way. The man's name was Sam, and for years afterward, whenever he heard the name Sam, our friend's first reaction was a sudden, sick feeling in the pit of his stomach. The trauma of that summer at camp remained with him, and unconsciously the name Sam took on a metamessage of cruelty and embarrassment.

In his book, *The Name Game,* Christopher P. Andersen cites a long list of names and the connotations or metasignals that he feels are behind them. Here are a few.

MASCULINE		FEMININE	
Name	*Metasignal*	*Name*	*Metasignal*
Abe	Manly, understanding	Amy	Active
Arthur	A bit lazy	Ann	Ladylike, honest, not pretty
Barry	Very masculine	Anita	Very sexy
Cyril	Sneaky	Alice	Simple, seemly
Daniel	Very virile	Betsy	Friendly, fun
Durwood	Insipid	Carole	Popular, vivacious
Garth	Forceful	Deanna	Exciting
George	Aggressive	Dotty	Bouncy
Hal	Industrious	Edith	Sexy
Hubert	Inert	Florence	Masculine
Jack	Diligent, very sexy	Ginny	Snappy
Johnny	A winner	Hildegarde	Lazy
Kermit	Unpopular	Isabel	Dull
Luke	Strong	Jennifer	Youthful, old-fashioned
Maurice	Dull	Lana	Alluring
Nathan	Vital	Mavis	Dull
Otis	A loner	Norma	Lonely
Preston	Solid	Patricia	Plain
Richard	Good-looking	Sabrina	Sultry
Saul	Strong	Toni	Energetic
Stanley	Dull	Vera	Predatory
Ted	Vigorous, popular	Yvonne	Stunning
Will	Average	Zelda	Aggressive

The list is fun to read, but the problem with names and their metasignals is that, much more than with words, their interpretation depends on personal experience. Andersen contends that Vera sends a signal of *predatory*. We know a Vera who is soft and charming. Vera says something entirely different to us.

Andersen bases the metasignals in his list on some broad polls across America. Whether he's right or wrong can be argued, but his basic premise, that names send out signals, is very true. We are all familiar with male names that send masculine signals, Chuck, Clint, Jim, Bob, Bill. The full names signal formality, Charles, Clinton, James, Robert, William. In TV programs we associate aggressive behavior with the metamessages of a single last name, Kojak, Colombo, Starsky, Hutch, McCloud—most of the names have a hard, clipped sound, a masculine sound. For the feminine sound of women's names we try for runs of *s*es and *l*s, Melissa, Sally, Alison, Lillian.

Children too play the name game, usually just for fun. In daydreams they take names that have private metamessages. After *Gone with the Wind* was made into a movie, how many young girls fantasized themselves as Scarlett? How many boys were Zorro or Mr. Spock? As adults, we still cherish secret names that spell out special qualities. "If only I had been born Daniel instead of Donald," a young man told us. Why? "I don't know except that Daniel seems so strong. Donald? I can only think of Donald Duck!"

A woman in her fifties confessed, "I always fantasize myself as Gabriella. Mysterious, beautiful! My given name, Ann, is too plain, too dull."

Many of us carry the daydreams into reality and change our name to one we feel is better suited to the person we really are, or the person we'd like to be. Then we try to live up to the name.

This has been done all through history, Andersen reminds us. The poet Petrarch started out as Francesco Petrarca. Bishop Fulton J. Sheen was Peter Sheen, a name that was evidently not strong enough for the career he had in mind. Jack Rosenberg became Werner Erhard and founded est, Erhard Sensitivity Training, a lucrative affair that might not have gotten off the ground as rst, Rosenberg Sensitivity Training.

Thomas W. Wilson took his middle name to become

Woodrow Wilson and Grover Cleveland dropped Stephen from his name. John Kennedy was always John or Jack, but his brothers were Bobby and Teddy. He was the President; they were the kid brothers.

After Watergate and an inaccessible President, the country was ripe for a candidate who projected the qualities of friendliness and familiarity. A Jimmy seemed to give us just that. The constant use of his first name, and a diminutive at that, sent out a metasignal of *the guy next door, someone you could talk to*. During the campaign and his first year in office we were swamped with Jimmy this and Jimmy that. Even his mother had a fund of stories about her Jimmy.

But as his first year in office wore on, subtle changes began to take place. More and more people referred to him not as Jimmy, or even Jimmy Carter, but as President Carter, and others simply Carter. What happened? Was it that as the man assumed the dignified office of President the diminutive did not match the grandeur of the post, or is it that Jimmy Carter has moved away from the people who elected him, become a little less accessible? And what will happen as his term ends and the new Presidential campaign starts? Will he assume the "down home" Jimmy image again, or will the image makers behind the scenes decide that we are ready for a President Carter or even a James Carter?

Inevitably the politician or public figure looks for a dynamic quality in his name instead of friendly familiarity or a commonplace sound. In Russia, during the revolution, Vladimir Ilich Ulyanov sounded far less dynamic than Nikolai Lenin, and Joseph Stalin was much stronger than Vissarionovich Dzhugashvili. Both Lenin and Stalin were easier to remember and easier for the non-Russian world to pronounce.

When we search out the original names of famous

people, it becomes fascinating to see the interaction between the metamessage of an assumed name and the way the man or woman sees himself or herself. In a sense we are all our own image makers. Some of us are tempted to change our names, and some follow through on the temptation. Most of us, however, live with our given names. They seem to be a part of us, as much a part as the color of our eyes or the shape of our heads. While we may secretly wish we had a prettier name, a stronger name, or a more formal name, there is, for most of us, the feeling that our name is so much a part of us that we are unwilling to give it up.

If you feel that way, yet are unhappy with your name, try a nickname. Assuming a nickname is much easier than changing your name legally. A good friend with the given name Elizabeth was much happier when she finally decided to change it to Betty. As a common nickname of Elizabeth she felt comfortable with it. To her, Betty was vibrant, Elizabeth old-fashioned.

Andersen, in his book lists Elizabeth as a seductive name. According to his poll, Betsy is friendly, Beth is animated, and Bess is motherly. We see Beth as soft and diffident; the memory of Beth in *Little Women* still haunts us, but we'll go along with friendly Betsy and motherly Bess.

8

Controlling the Feedback

THE AUTOMATIC RESPONSE

A very common word game is Automatic Response. You play this game without thinking. You're asked a question, and you reply with a quick answer. What you hope to do with your answer is cut off communication. The game is closely linked to masking and isolation.

Someone shoves against you in the market and says, "Sorry." Your Automatic Response is, "It's all right." The sense of the words is placating, but all too often the metasignal you send out is *annoyance. How could you be so clumsy?* In the circumstances you feel an annoyed response is not proper, so you mask your annoyance—or try to mask it. In this situation, an interaction between strangers, the masking is a social formula.

But the same situation at home, between a father and child, is far from neutral. The child, running through the room, bumps into his father. He sings out,

"Sorry!" but the father is annoyed, and it shows in his "It's all right." The child senses the controlled annoyance and feels that it isn't all right.

Bewildered and uneasy, he responds with "I didn't mean it."

If, at this point, the father becomes aware of his child's metamessage, the troubled emotion behind the words, he might hesitate, bend down, and in a comforting voice reassure the child, explaining his annoyance. But this supposes a degree of sensitivity most busy fathers don't have. The usual reaction is irritation at the child's continued apology, and a masking of that irritation.

Inevitably this kind of masking is damaging to any relationship. The resentment the father holds in is not dissipated. It remains to become a barrier against any real feelings, and he becomes isolated behind it.

The Automatic Response needn't be an apologetic "I'm sorry" or "It's all right." It can be any part of a bitter exchange, an answer to the pointing finger of blame. A husband does something wrong and his wife says "It's all your fault."

Without really absorbing the accusation or thinking about it, he comes back with "I didn't do anything!" The root of the problem is never unearthed. He might have said, "Why is it my fault?" or "What could I do to prevent it?" or "How else could I have acted?" Any of these answers might have exposed the situation, but they aren't automatic. The answer the husband chose, "I didn't do anything," was not true. He may not have done what he was accused of, but he was at fault. The point is to find out why.

To answer automatically is to raise a barrier. The only recourse the wife has is to continue the attack. "You never think" or "You're always on his side" or "You did it to hurt me." The attack is allowed, even invited, because "I didn't do anything," a defensive communication, is contradicted by a negative metasignal. It is not said defensively, but aggressively, provocatively.

Another automatic exchange often occurs between lovers once the bloom is off the romance. "What's bothering you now?" The communication is concern, but the metacommunication is *long-suffering patience*. The accent is on *now*, not on *bothering*. The automatic response is usually a sullen "Nothing." But something *is* bothering the lover, very obviously, and it has come across in all the metasignals that accompany what she's saying. She has just never clearly said what *is* wrong.

When she's challenged by her lover, her automatic response is "Nothing." This masking device only serves to isolate her from him. The fear of disclosing the truth, of saying just what it is that's troubling her, is tied up with a fear of rejection. She is firmly convinced that it isn't safe to express her feelings. If she does, she will be too vulnerable, too easily hurt, and yet she isn't prepared to carry the masking to its logical extreme and hide the fact that she is hurt. She has to send that *hurt* out as a clue to her lover. The metamessage here is a rather desperate *Understand, know I'm being hurt, and help me*. But the message is masked and doomed to end in isolation.

The Automatic Response is firmly locked into our unconscious behavior. Here are some typical questions along with the automatic responses that usually answer them.

"What are you doing?" "Nothing."

"What are you thinking about?" "Nothing."

"Where are you going?" "I don't know."

"How do you feel?" "Okay" or "Fine."

You can add dozens more to the list once you begin

to think about it. In every case the answer is automatic and communicates nothing on the surface. But there is a world of meaning in its metamessage. We attempt to mask, but unconsciously we let our true feelings leak through. In essence, we use the metalevel to communicate.

Is there any way we can refuse to play the Automatic Response game? Is there any way we can bring the hidden messages up to the surface, match our communication to our metacommunication, and take off the mask? If we can do it successfully, and convince our partner to do it, we can avoid isolation, hurt, neglect, and misunderstanding.

The first step is really to listen to the question, to consider it, to hold back the automatic response while we think about our answer. When we do answer, let it reflect how we really feel.

Answer the man who jostles you and says, "I'm sorry," with "I know you couldn't help it, but it upset me. I'll get over it in a minute or two."

"It's all your fault" can be answered with a rational explanation or question. "What do you think I should have done?" or "I was trying to do so and so." The discussion won't stop at that. It's bound to go on, but you can express the way you honestly feel, and in turn find out how your partner feels.

Sometimes the question becomes an intrusion on your privacy. "What are you thinking about?" could be answered with "I was into some very private thoughts. I'd rather not talk about them."

The honesty of your answer will get across. There may be a continuing discussion, but it will make sense. The other person may be hurt if you're truthful, but he'll still be likely to respect your privacy. At least you haven't hidden behind a meaningless automatic response. Ill will or anger may come up, but they will come up on the surface. It's as important to express your anger as it is to hide it by saying, "I didn't want to hurt his feelings."

Even when you do hide what you really feel, some of it is bound to leak out. You never do a complete job of masking. The mask rarely sits that securely. Even the "Nothing" answer conveys a wealth of information in its metasignals: unhappiness, despair, self-pity.

The problem, of course, is that being completely honest in your answer is not easy. Honesty leads to unmasking, and while unmasking can be a good thing, it can also be difficult and painful as well.

Sometimes it's a good idea to unmask gradually. You might start by giving the standard automatic response, but change the metamessage behind the words. Instead of saying "Nothing" and sending out sullen metasignals, try "Nothing" in a joking tone, a gentle tone, a sympathetic tone—in as many different shades of meaning as you can manage. It's a first step toward unmasking. Once you've mastered this, you may move on to genuine communication as well as genuine metacommunication.

THE POWER GAME

"When I want a thing, I get it, even though I let everyone have their say," Mr. Sloan told his son when he took him into the business. "You can learn how to manage people if you watch the way I go about it."

But after a month of watching his father, young Sloan informed him that he was going back to college. "I'm going for a masters in geologic engineering, Dad. I don't belong in business."

"Why not?"

He looked at his father speculatively. "To tell the truth, I just can't play the games you do."

Mr. Sloan was hurt. "I don't play games. You tell me what games I play. There's the monthly meeting with the staff today. You come along and see if I play games—games! Those dodos just don't cooperate."

His son went along to the meeting and took notes as well. That evening he tried to explain to his father what had gone on. "You know, Dad, you played an out-and-out power game."

"Me? Ridiculous! How?"

Young Sloan looked at his notes. "You walked into that meeting, and the first thing you said was, 'I got your report, Jack. It needs work.' Then you turned to Roger and told him, 'You can do what you like, but put out that cigarette.' And to Al, 'We need more sales ideas, and I want them better than the last batch.' Do you realize what you were doing?"

"I wasn't wrong. The report needed work. I'm allergic to smoke and nobody submits ideas that are usable."

"But you never give anyone a chance to present any ideas. Your tone of voice makes it clear that the only ideas you want are your own. You've got the power and you use it."

"That's pretty big talk from a kid who's still wet behind the ears!"

"There! You're doing it with me now. It's a perfect put-down. You try to prove that I don't know anything so that you can ridicule anything I say."

"You're making me out to be some kind of an ogre. Look, I'm fair to my employees," Mr. Sloan blustered.

"We're not talking fair. We're talking power. You told the meeting you were open for suggestions, but in your opinion—and then you spelled out what you wanted them to do. That's a power play. Don't you see that? You ask them for something, but your voice lets them know you don't really want it."

After a long, thoughtful pause, Mr. Sloan said, "So tell me about the job opportunities in geologic engineering."

The power game Mr. Sloan played can be summed up very easily. Step one: a simple statement that disarms the opponent. Step two: a killer blow that cuts off communication. Along with these two steps, he fostered the illusion that he was open to suggestion, but since no one dared to come up with one he had to step in himself.

To be played properly the game requires a strong attack. This throws the opponent off balance, and it must be followed up quickly with a statement of what you want. To be effective, the aggressive player must have the necessary clout to both attack and follow up.

The words used in the power game are important, but the metamessage behind the words tells the true story. Mr. Sloan, at the meeting that lost him his son as a partner, told his employees that he was open to suggestions, but in the next breath he added, "In *my* opinion there is only *one* way to go about this." The emphasis on *my* made it clear that this was a directive As if this were not enough, he added the fact that there was only *one* way, again an emphasis that didn't allow for contradiction.

The power game, we've stressed, needs clout, and therefore it's a perfect game for a boss like Mr. Sloan But it can also be played successfully within a family. Here Dad is usually the aggressor.

"We'll talk it over, but no daughter of mine is staying out after one o'clock!" or "Sure we can discuss it, but I want the car washed this afternoon" or

"Make whatever you want for dinner, but don't expect me to eat any fish."

Sometimes Mom initiates the game. "Of course she's a nice girl, but I don't think she's right for you." Or, when the game is played between lovers, "You're a sexy girl, but you could use a little more meat on those bones." The end objective of the game is always to put down the other player and assert your own power.

There is an offshoot of this game that is concerned with power in a subtler way. Here, the object is to put the other player down by exposing him to submerged guilts. It's played best when you reach that point in a relationship where some important truths are beginning to surface. The player who initiates the game simulates complete dismay and says, "I just can't take it when you shout at me."

Even when no shouting has been done, this kind of statement is loaded with metasignals that remind the other player that he is a beast, a bully, and should feel as guilty as hell.

The man can initiate the game too if he gets there first. "You must think I'm a louse!" The guilt is turned around, and the woman becomes the one at fault for harboring such thoughts. His metasignals tell her he's crushed, and she has no alternative except to protest, "No. I don't think that of you at all." The power is right back in his corner!

THE BLAME GAME

When Judd and Wilma fight, Wilma always has the last word. "The point is," Judd says wryly, "she gets me into this situation where all I'm doing is protesting." How does she do it? Very simply. She plays the Blame Game

This is a tricky little semantic game that rarely fails It depends on the metamessage behind key words, words such as *uptight, cool, excited*. When an argument gets to the point where Wilma can't think of a rejoinder, she initiates the game. She tells Judd, "Don't get uptight," or "Don't get excited," or "You're losing your cool," or even, "You're over reacting "

Judd pulls back at once, trying to excuse what he's said and how he said it. He begins to doubt not only himself but also his position. Was he excited, overreacting, losing his cool? The words Wilma chose have deep metasignals for Judd. He belongs to a generation that desperately wanted to stay *cool* at all costs that hated being *uptight*. His sudden pause to re-examine what he's said gives Wilma the edge in the argument and he's lost!

The principle behind this game is blame You blame the other player and put the condition you choose *excited, overreacting, whatever,* on him, forcing him to defend himself, to prove he's none of the things he's accused of To be played successfully, you must know the other player intimately enough to understand what key words hold significant metamessages for him It's a perfect game for lovers!

Lovers, in any case, are great game players—often to the point where the love affair is totally destroyed It's as if they had to flex their linguistic muscles for the coming marriage They may unconsciously reason "If we can endure each other's games and even win a few perhaps we have a good chance of taying together "

One classic lover's game is the Sexual Game It's structured around performance The player who ini tiates the first move masks his play with profuse concern. It should take place immediately after a sexual encounter.

"Was everything all right?" Metamessage of *concern.*

"Of course. Why do you ask?" Metamessage of *faint anxiety.*

"You seemed—I don't know—were you feeling all right?" Metamessage of *awkwardness.*

"What do you mean, all right? Look, didn't *you* enjoy it?" Metamessage of *deepening anxiety.*

"Oh, me? Well—I was worried about you." Metamessage of *evasion.*

"You mean you didn't!" Metamessage of *full-blown anxiety.*

"Look, let's drop it." Metamessage of *concern.*

"No, come on. What did I do wrong?" And they're away and ready for a real knock-down-drag-out. The point of the game is to convince the other player, without coming out and saying so, that he/she didn't perform just right. The best way to do it is with deep concern over his/her enjoyment. This plants doubt in his/her mind about your enjoyment. The metasignals are extremely delicate and important here because, without them, the game could be mistaken for genuine concern.

Another lovers' game is the Helplessness Ploy. This is based on a deep understanding of aggression, and it involves the use of genetic turnoffs, instinctive appeasing gestures. Just try to bawl out someone who turns up his hands and says, in a genuinely humble voice, "I'm sorry. I was all wrong." The gesture and the words, both metasignals of apology, are enough to defuse hostility. The hostile emotion, though defused, is still there, and it must be handled somehow. The usual method is to turn it into frustration.

As the game is played, one lover says, "Why did you do it? You know how upset I get."

A healthy reaction would be "No, I didn't know" or "I did it for this and that reason" or "Why are you upset about it?" But that wouldn't be playing the game. To play, the other lover must use the Helplessness Ploy and say, "I didn't mean it. I'm sorry."

This is an appeasing statement and her lover's anger is defused, but unfortunately still there gnawing away in frustration. It's an uncomfortable game, especially if it happens again and again, and it's a dangerous one because the anger must come out eventually. All too often it surfaces in an angry reaction or a violent confrontation and separation. The game is hardly worth the winning.

THE NO GAME

The No Game depends on the use of words of denial or refusal, on negatives. Usually these are accompanied by metasignals of anger or criticism, put-downs or imperatives. The No Game can be devastating when it is used against someone who is vulnerable or unable to fight back.

Children are usually the victims in this game of verbal assault. The adult world of parents and teachers uses negatives without discrimination when it deals with children. In a family, a child depends on his parents for care and protection, guidance, love, and understanding. He is not only vulnerable and dependent, but powerless as well.

Maryanne is only five, but she is already a victim of the No Game. When her mother talks to her, it's with a barrage of negatives. "Don't do that. Stop annoying the baby. No, you can't go out. You mustn't play with the stove, the sink, the dishes. Don't hurt yourself. Don't go out of the yard," and so on and on.

Mother is overworked, and she uses a tense, sharp tone and an angry voice to accentuate her commands. Maryanne reacts by trying to please her mother. Perhaps, if she does nothing at all, her mother won't be so angry. But even this doesn't work. "Don't sit around. Don't be idle. Don't look so beaten!"

Finally, when the barrage of *don'ts, stops, can'ts* and *mustn'ts* gets to be too much, Maryanne begins to take the only defense she knows. She tunes out her mother's voice and retreats into a private little shell.

"I don't understand the child," her mother complains to her father. "She never listens to me, and she's always daydreaming. It can't be healthy."

Maryanne's playmate, Billy, lives down the block, and his father plays the No Game too. Most of his conversation with his small son is delivered in a belittling voice. "Don't play with your sister's dolls!"

Guiltily, Billy drops the doll. He hears the disapproving metasignal in his father's voice, and he knows he's done something wrong. Boys should not play with dolls. He is not measuring up to what his father wants.

Later, at the dinner table, Father lets go with a few more damaging negative metamessages. "Don't eat with your elbows on the table. Don't talk with your mouth full. Stop fidgeting. Eat, don't play around with your food."

Billy gulps and tears well up in his eyes. He fights them back, but his father has seen them. "And don't act like a baby. Big boys don't cry." This goes on and on until Billy rushes away from the table. When his mother goes after him, he starts throwing a tantrum.

Afterward his father says, "Why can't he behave like other kids? He's always on the edge of tears."

Hearing negative messages over and over again, children like Maryanne and Billy begin to adopt their parents' words and metasignals as their own. They tell themselves, "I'm not a good person. I'm so bad, even my father and mother can't love me."

When the No Game is played with an Ask and Tell routine, it carries twice the impact of the No Game alone. Jane, a teenager, is trying to zip up a skirt that is a bit too tight around the waist. Her mother watches for a moment, then clicks her tongue in disgust and says, "Why can't you cut out the candy bars? Why can't you show a little more control?" Jane hears the words and picks up the metasignals behind them and suddenly she feels fat and ugly.

"Can't you figure out anything for yourself?" Arnold's father asks him. What started out as a father-son project to fix the family car ends right there. Arnold is not only hurt but paralyzed by his father's critical tone. He's heard it just about every time he tried to do something. After a while, he thinks, "Dad must be right. I can't figure anything out. I must be plain stupid!"

Children are not the only victims in the No Game with an Ask and Tell variation. Between husbands and wives or between lovers the game often reaches epidemic proportions. "Why can't you get anywhere on time?" "Couldn't you remember just once?" Or that tired old one, "Why don't you ever want to make love when I do?"

The negative question is filled with metacues. Usually sarcasm and criticism, irony and contempt are part of the slick packaging of the verbal message. First there is the question, a question that doesn't really want an answer. The question tells the other player that you are out to hurt, punish, or attack. If you are challenged, you can always step back and slip into the safety of "I was only asking."

The receiver of such a question has limited choices. She can either be defensive, guilty, tune out, or send back a few negative messages of her own. Then the two are bombarding each other with "Why can't you . . ." "You never . . ." "You shouldn't . ." "You don't . . ." "How could you . . ." The game plays to a draw, but such exchanges will often escalate into violent verbal arguments.

A child may be helpless when confronted with the No Game, but an adult is less vulnerable. There are things you can say, not to win the game but to abort it. If you're on the receiving end, you must first be aware that you are the victim of such behavior. Refuse to play it out. Learn to confront the other player with a direct statement.

In a firm voice say, "Tell me just what you mean when you say I never want to make love when you do. Maybe we can work it out." Or, "I hear the anger and sarcasm in your voice when you tell me I'm never on time, and I find it hard to talk about it when you speak to me that way."

Finally, listen to all the metasignals that go along with Ask and Tell. Do the signals have a familiar ring? Metacommunication, like the language itself, is handed down from one generation to another. All of us remember and use again the vocal mannerisms of our parents, and when we come to choose a husband or wife, we look for someone who'll treat us the way dear old Mom or Dad did.

If they treated us with love and respect, we'll tend to pick partners who use positive metamessages, but if our parents played the No Game with us, we'll often look for a partner to continue the game playing.

If your partner plays the No Game with you, ask yourself if it is the same game your parents played. If it is, you may be equally responsible for the game playing. Or, if you are the one to initiate the game, are you simply carrying on an old family tradition?

Once you are aware of the reasons behind the game, it becomes easier to stop the game or to refuse to play it out to its logical conclusion. You must remember that none of these games played by lovers, families, or friends are really worth the playing. There are no winners of them, only losers, but too often we realize this too late. The game destroys relationships by destroying communication with ugly metacommunication.

9

Program Changes

THE CHANGING TERMS

Metacommunication, like body language, is tied to the culture we grow up in and the language we learn to speak. The metasignals of Italy are very different from those of England or the United States, and all are different from those of Spain, France, or Israel.

Italians, for example, are more eloquent, and use greater varieties of stress, tone, and volume in their speech. Without understanding Italian, it is still possible to get a good idea of what an Italian is saying by picking up some of the metasignals in his voice and by watching his hands, face, and body gestures.

The English and Scandinavians use metasignals that are more subdued, less eloquent. Their voice sings a different melody, and like their body language, their metacommunication is subtler, with harder-to-decipher signals, and it usually tells us little beyond the meaning of the words.

Metacommunication varies from country to country, but it can also vary within a country. Southerners will have one set of signals, Northerners another. Mountain folk use one type of stress, valley folk a different kind, and with all this variation, the language itself is in a constant process of change.

As we have seen in previous chapters, slang and jargon float in and out of the language, some staying to become part of our speech, others enjoying a brief vogue and then disappearing. Ordinary words are lost, meanings change, and in changing send out different signals in different times to different parts of the country.

Yankee is a term of pride in New England, but down South it's an unpleasant label. To one generation, grass is something to smoke; to another, it's something to weed and mow. It was only a few generations back that the blacks in the United States were referred to as colored. By the thirties and forties the term Negro gradually replaced colored. In many parts of the country black and white children grew up feeling the rightness of Negro. It gave dignity to a race, and it allowed its developing consciousness to understand and take pride in its achievements. The metasignals behind it were positive.

Then, in the sixties, the term black was adopted by the Negro people themselves. To whites and to many blacks the metasignals behind the word were harsh and discordant. It had always seemed insulting to characterize someone by their color. Now black was a militant source of pride and identification for a people!

Today, in the late seventies, for most of us black is a comfortable term. Negro seems old-fashioned, even patronizing, while colored is completely insensitive. But what has changed? Why do one generation's positive metasignals become the next generation's negative signals?

The answer lies in the strength of the link between metacommunication and social change, and since social change is uneven, remnants of the old terms, colored, Negro, are still used in many parts of the country. To some they remain a more comfortable form, to others they are a racist slur.

The regional and racial differences in metacommunication are obvious to all of us, but increasingly we are being made aware of another difference, the difference in metacommunication between the sexes.

For years only an enlightened few were aware of the sexist nature of communication and metacommunication. But as the feminist movement gained momentum, many women and some men began to challenge what they considered the sexist slant of our language.

One very pervasive example of this is the generic use of *man* to mean all human beings. To a young man growing up in our society, generic man is easy enough to understand. "Sure, man means all of us." All of us? A young woman is not quite so certain that it applies to her too, and no amount of reassurance can completely erase the metasignals that tell her that *man* or *men* relate chiefly to the male sex. She may be familiar with the Declaration of Independence and know that it says "all men are created equal." But the words mean one thing to men, another to women.

The truth is, when the document was written women were not included. They were not legally men's equal. Today, though many of us choose to understand that the *men* in the Declaration is a generic term, we know that economically, socially, and legally women may have come a "long way, baby," but they still have a long way to go toward equality.

THINKING MALE

The use of *man* in the English language is all pervasive. Some attempts to correct the situation have resulted in changing chairman to chairperson, salesman to salesperson, and spokesman to spokesperson. Clumsy as they may sound to ears attuned to the old metasignals, the changes are increasingly successful and seem here to stay. And yet *man* invades the language on so many levels. A young lady in Babylon, New York, fretted over her name, Ellen Cooperman, just so long, and then legally changed it to Ellen Cooperperson! Foolish? No. Not if the metasignals behind Cooperman were too disturbing to her.

The fact is that in most cases, when we use the word *man,* we don't think of humanity in general. We think *male*. This was proved in a study at Drake University. Chapter headings for a supposed textbook were given to over three hundred students who were then asked to select pictures from magazines and newspapers to illustrate the chapters.

The students were divided into two groups, and one group was given chapter headings such as *Political Man, Industrial Man,* and *Economic Man*. The other group had chapter headings that read *Political Life, Industrial Life,* and *Economic Behavior*.

The selection of pictures proved that the metasignals behind *man,* even when it was used in the generic sense to mean humanity, are exclusively male. As an example, for the heading *Economic Man,* the students chose pictures showing men in economic situations, men at desks in their offices, at a stock exchange, in a bank.

When they chose pictures for the heading *Economic Behavior*, however, they selected those which showed women and children in various economic situations. The sociologists who initiated the study concluded that images such as male bankers, male politicians, or male workers are suggested by the word *man*. The words *behavior* and *life* suggested women and children to the students.

As an answer to the question, Why is *man* always associated with male? the researchers suggest that the metasignals attached to the word *man*—man equals male—arise early in life before the child learns the generic concept of *man*. Once the connection has been made between man and male, it becomes locked into the child's unconscious. Children may understand the generic use of *man* once they begin to read, but by then it's too late.

The same early connection is made between the word *he* and male. Later, children are told *he* can be generic and refer to both sexes, but by then the association is firmly locked into the unconscious.

From birth to death, we carry our sexual identity with us. A baby boy becomes a little boy, a big boy, and finally a man. Until recently, it has been little girl, big girl, and then—just girl. Seldom, before the feminine awareness movement took place, did many girls graduate into women. The housewife had her cleaning girl, no matter that she was well over forty. The businessman had a girl for a secretary, and when women got together to shop or go to a matinee, it was always the "girls" who were out for the day. Women as well as men used the term freely.

Today, the term *girl* is looked upon by many as an insult, a refusal to admit them to adulthood. The metasignals behind *woman* are strong, but behind *girl* they hear condescension and inferiority, the classic "male chauvinist put-down."

Other women, however, pick up different metasignals from *girl*. "It makes me feel young, kind of cute and—well, desirable—to be called a girl," one woman admitted to us. "I mean, who wants to be thought of as a forty-year-old woman?"

Another woman in her late twenties was even more frank. "I know I should want to be called a woman, but when I hear the word applied to me personally, I feel vulnerable, like I'm just not that ready to be that grown up."

And so we have two extremes in reaction to a simple noun. And in between there are the majority of women who are unsure of what to call themselves. Again, the problem lies in the close connection between language and social progress.

A WOMAN'S LANGUAGE

As we become aware of the sexism that underlies the man-woman relationship in our culture, we can make the connection between sociosexual development and sexism not only in our language but also in our concepts about our language.

Men and women, it is generally believed, speak a different language, and most people hold that the speech of women is less effective than that of men. The melody, volume, and tone of their voices are less confident, weaker than those of men. Because of this, the theory goes, radio and television newscasters have, until recently, been men. For a while, several years back, it was acceptable to have a weatherwoman. After all, weather was not as serious as the domestic or foreign news.

Now, slowly, women are making headway in full news coverage, and they seem to be the equals of men in the fields of metacommunication and communication. But the old traditions die slowly, and a Barbara Walters is mimicked for her lisp while the rude, abrasive metacommunication of a Mike Wallace is looked on as tough reporting.

Using the yardstick of economic progress, few would argue that it is the men who hold the power. In business, most corporation heads are men, and the same applies in politics and the top government jobs. Men, even in comparable jobs, make more money than women, and on the homefront, while Mother seems to be in charge, Father holds the most powerful weapon of all, the purse strings.

In the sexual arena, in spite of all the new freedom, it is still the man who chooses and the woman who waits to be chosen. While this inequality exists, the metasignals of men and women are bound to be different. The man will have a more aggressive voice, a louder and more confident voice, and women will send out signals of submission, availability, and vulnerability.

But as we change, as women begin to see themselves as capable and independent, both sexes will hear new metasignals behind the others' voices.

Cheris Kramer, an instructor in speech communication at the University of Illinois, set out to uncover the existing metasignals behind our voices. She initiated an elaborate study to discover what differences there were between the ways men and women spoke.

First she decided to analyze the mythology that maintains that there is a difference. She used cartoons because she saw them as representative of "Folk Linguistics," the generally accepted folklore about the language.

The cartoonists, predominantly men, gave the impression, in their drawings, that women spoke less often, in fewer places, and were incapable of handling the language properly. Men, in the cartoons, swore more often and were simpler and more direct and assertive in using the language. This, she concluded, was the popular mythology about women's speech, a mythology propagated by men.

To get at the truth, Kramer compared compositions written by men and women about the same subject. After a careful analysis, she concluded that *none of the supposed differences existed!* If our society views female speech as inferior, she said, "It is because of the subordinate role assigned to women."

But in her study there was one important clue. "A greater number of sex differences," she pointed out, "may exist in *spoken* than in *written* language." This is another way of saying that on the metacommunicative level, there are many sex differences. What are these differences?

Dorothy Uris, in her book *A Woman's Voice,* analyzes some of these differences on the metalevel. Uris, a voice coach and former actress, lists first the "high childish accents" that sometimes persist into middle age. The metamessage she reads into such voices is *Don't expect too much of me.*

The voice that is listless, with a breathy, trailing tone, signals, *I am housebound, exhausted from lack of adult contact.* The supersoft, ladylike intonation signals, *I should be seen and not heard.* The flat, nasal sound and monotonous rhythm is linked to premature age, *I am old before my time.* Shrill verbal aggression, Uris says, signals frustration while a sultry, smooth voice is synonymous with sex.

Uris suggests a series of vigorous breathing exercises and extended voice training as the answer to all these problems. It takes work to communicate with clear words linked together in a line of clear tones, she insists. But again, all this seems suspiciously like another aspect of linguistic folklore. Are women's voices really so much in need of remedial help? The difficulties in metacommunication that Uris cites could just as easily be applied to men. Many male voices are unpleasant, aggressively harsh or flat and nasal. It may well be that what Uris sees as a problem in women's voices is again part of the subordinate role women have been taught to play in our culture.

THE POLITE SEX

Whatever Uris and Kramer say about the speech quality of men and women, the question remains: Is there a difference in the way the two sexes use the language? Is there a difference besides the physiological qualities of the male and female voice?

In *Language and Women's Place,* Robin Lakoff of the University of California at Berkeley has attributed a special language to women. This language, according to Lakoff, sends out signals of indecision, uncertainty, hesitancy, and subordination.

How does women's language differ from men's? Lakoff suggests some typical devices women use. One is the insistence on a tag question. Instead of a simple statement such as "The food is terrible," the kind of statement a man might make to his wife in a restaurant, a woman will usually say, "The food is terrible, isn't it?" The *isn't it* is the tag question, as if she stepped back objectively in order to disassociate her-

itant, waiting to be told what to do, and *reluctant to take risks.*

To compete successfully in the man's world, they must change, and the first order of change must be in their language. They must lose their hesitancy, stop answering a question with a question, avoid using tag questions, and forget about politeness. All this must go if they are to be successful. The metasignals behind their words must be clear and positive, asking rather than pleading, stating instead of suggesting.

Some time back Norman Lear, who has brought so many popular series to television, ushered in something called "All That Glitters." It was a sitcom in which the traditional roles were reversed. Women managed big business and men were secretaries or househusbands. The series bombed rather quickly, not so much because it was a one-joke deal—what sitcom isn't?—but because of the awkward acting, stale gags, and the fact that the actors and script lacked conviction.

This lack of conviction was one of the curious things about the failure of the show. It seemed to happen because of the inability of many of the women playing dominant roles to capture the speech patterns of dominance, and the failure of the men to assume subordinate women's speech patterns. There was evidently a confusion about sexuality, dominance, femininity and masculinity. The pitch, resonance, volume, and tone—all the physical elements that give one sex the upper hand—were forgotten. The women still talked as women talk in a male-dominated society, and even the choice of words, the commands and orders that women gave, lacked the traditional arrogance of men.

Nowadays, as women fight for social equality, their language becomes freer, more the equal of men's.

Many answer questions with statements instead of questions, leave off tag questions, and are direct instead of overly polite. Some are even using obscenity as freely as men do.

Parents of college girls, unable to see their linguistic freedom as a reflection of general equality, throw up their hands in horror at the use of four-letter words "Today's kids are going down the drain. There's a breakdown of morals, and their language . !"

If they understood the reasons behind the apparent looseness of speech they might feel that far from a breakdown in morality, the free speech could be showing a higher morality, a morality of equality. On the other hand, it is also possible that the ubiquitous use of four-letter words is one generation's hostility and revolt against the Establishment. Obscene speech, for many young women, is an expression of freedom. Today, for better or worse, profanity has become more acceptable in the language, and the metasignals behind it seem to have lost much of their intensity

But whatever steps young women take to change things, the fact is that men are still calling the shots They still dominate women, at least when a man and woman are alone and talking. Pamela Fishman of the University of California at Santa Barbara proved this in a recent experiment. She analyzed fifty-two hours of tapes made in the apartments of three middle-class couples between the ages of twenty-five and thirty five

In spite of the fact that the couples knew they were being taped, the men still controlled the conversation "Men control topics by veto as well as by positive effort," Fishman noted. This was true even though the women raised twice as many topics of conversation as the men The men simply refused to respond to those topics they didn't like

When the women were faced with grunts and long silences from the men, they responded by resorting to attention-getting devices. They asked three times as many questions as the men did, and they prefaced their talk with introductory remarks such as, "Do you know what?" or "This is interesting."

When talk lagged, the women began to interject "You know" into the conversation more and more often. While men used these same devices if their talk failed, they usually didn't have to. As a rule, the women responded enthusiastically whenever the men spoke.

THE USE OF OBSCENITY

One of the problems faced by women when they try to use obscenity is the vast history of male dominance, a history that has allowed men to evolve an entire vocabulary about women, and an ugly vocabulary at that. No such vocabulary exists for women. They simply do not have the words to express real anger and hostility. What term can a woman use to put a man down? She can call him a stud, a stallion, a bull, a womanizer, a Don Juan, a pimp, a beast, a lecher, a brute—but so many of these are semicomplimentary and carry positive metasignals. A macho-type man swells his chest with pride if he is called a stud or a stallion by a woman. It's no insult from a male-dominated point of view.

But consider the other side of the coin, the words reserved for women in the male vocabulary. Bitch, cow, dog, mouse, pig, vixen, chick, pussy (so many animals!) or a broad, a piece of ass, a piece of tail, a cunt—the list is overwhelming. None of these labels can even remotely make a woman proud. They are contemptuous, denigrating, and hostile.

A recent attempt was made by a group of feminists to change the meaning of *bitch* and give women a sense of pride in the word. The term, they noted, was applied to a dog in estrus when she was aggressive, defensive, and offensive. Why not take pride in these attributes? It was a nice try, but it didn't work. For most women, the metasignals behind the word bitch are just too strong. It will take a lot more than self-pride to change them.

In fact, when we wish to insult a man we'll call him a son of a bitch, but the insult is to his mother, a feminine put-down. In the same way, calling him a bastard reflects on his mother.

The use of obscenity by men toward women is a clear indication of hostility, and it is so pervasive that most men are not aware of it even when it is pointed out to them. It seems the normal way of speech.

But why should men show such hostility to women? We get a hint of an answer when we consider the military training of men, particularly in an elite organization like the Marine Corps. In his book, *Sex and Suicide,* George Gilder writes about the way recruits were treated at Parris Island, the Marine boot camp. The trainees were subjected to a constant flood of abuses, and everything that is despicable was labeled feminine. If they showed any weakness, they were threatened with "Act like a cunt and I'll treat you like a cunt!"

Gilder says that "virtually every sentence, every description, every lesson embodies this sexual duality, and the female anatomy provides a rich metaphor for every degradation." The reason? He suggests that when you want to create a group of male killers, you first kill the woman in them.

But to a minor extent the same training is given all men in our society, the same contempt for the female body, for anything feminine. It's drummed into men at a very early age. We don't need Marine boot camp to tell us that when a boy acts like a girl he is considered despicable. Feminine emotions and attitudes are held in contempt. A violent contempt for women is found in street gangs, in the ghetto, among blue-collar bachelors, and among some groups of college men. The fellowship of men, the bonding of men, not only locks out the female but also encourages contempt for her. And if any woman tries to break into that special male society, the same obscenity that "kills the woman" in these men is used to attack the interloper.

This is so blatant that the United States Labor Department in April of 1977 drafted a series of proposed regulations "to insure and maintain a working environment free of harassment, intimidation, and coercion."

The men in construction work, as an example, saw the women coming into the field as threats and reacted not only with physical violence but also with obscene verbal abuse. And the verbal abuse, a number of women construction workers insist, is as bad as any threat of physical violence.

"It's a constant harassment. Never mind the graffiti they scribble all over. That can make my blood boil," one woman construction worker told us. "But the hardest thing to take is the verbal assault, the macho catcalls that make you realize you're no more than a body to them, not a person."

What it boils down to is that for many men their own sexual identity depends on subjugating women, if not physically, then with words, and with all the metasignals behind the words.

It's not only working men who go in for verbal

harassment. Listen in on a group of white-collar workers, executives, and whatnots, as they stand around the water cooler. They eye a young secretary as she passes, and one of them says in a carrying voice, "Man, that's stacked!"

There's a laugh from the others and the woman turns around. "I don't appreciate that kind of remark!"

The man who spoke pretends surprise, and in an innocent voice says, "Remark? I wasn't talking about you. I was discussing those stacked journals."

The woman knows he's lying. The remark was addressed to his friends and to her as well. It was meant to embarrass her, to throw her off balance and make her vulnerable. Even though she was assertive enough to challenge him, she knew the odds were against her. If she continued to make a fuss, she'd be "overreacting" or too "sensitive."

Later, in the same office, a supervisor comes out to give the receptionist at the main desk some papers. He leans over her and in a low, suggestive voice says, "Nice sweater, Betty." Betty blushes. She hears the way he drags out the word nice, and drops his voice at sweater. The sexual message is clear.

The supervisor is not complimenting Betty on her taste in sweaters. He's making a sexual remark about her breasts. From past experience she knows that if she challenges him he'll back out of it neatly. "I was paying a compliment." Then, in a suggestive tone, "What did you think I meant?"

In this type of harassment, the blame for a sexual metamessage is placed firmly on the victim. If you understand the metacommunication, you're guilty. Such harassment is not unusual in the working world. Last year *Redbook* magazine took a survey of sexual harassment on the job. They polled nine thousand working women and reported that 92 percent of them cited verbal sexual abuse, communicated directly or indirectly, as the leading cause of embarrassment, shame, and even fear on the job.

Most of the women were white-collar workers, but there were many professionals and blue-collar workers too. The women were of every age and class. The most common harassment was verbal, a comment on a woman's looks or a dirty joke, sometimes an outright demand for sex.

The problem in all this use of obscenity was summed up by authors Casey Miller and Kate Swift in their book, *Words and Women*. "To the degree that words, as we customarily use them, minimize the humanity of women and maximize their status as objects, we are all—female and male—the losers."

In their book, Miller and Swift make some suggestions about "cleaning up the language" we use and so changing the metasignals behind the words. They suggest that we stop using *he* in the generic sense and try the plural usage, *they, them, their*. They would do away with *-ess* endings in words such as Jewess, Negress, poetess, and the *-ette* endings in such words as *farmerette, astronette*. They recommend *Ms*. to balance *Mr*., and suggest *forewoman, congresswoman,* and *newspaperwoman*, where the titles are applicable.

Terms like *forefather* they would replace with *ancestor; man,* in the generic sense, by *human being;* and they would reverse the typical order of man and woman, boy and girl with an occasional Eve and Adam, daughters and sons and so on.

But they do admit that it is an overwhelming job, and of course the first step is to make people aware of the sexist nature of the language. Neutral terms such as chairperson seem awkward now, the metasignals confusing, but metasignals can change quickly and in a few years chairman may seem equally awkward to us.

Whatever the change in terminology, the very important change must be in the metasignals behind the word. The word womanly is a good case in point. The word *manly* is its masculine parallel, and in *Webster's New Collegiate Dictionary, manly* is defined as having qualities generally associated with a man: STRONG, VIRILE. By contrast, *womanly* is defined as having qualities characteristic of a woman.

The full definition of *manly* is energetic, vigorous (the dictionary definition of virile), and strong. *Womanly,* however, is no more or less than being a woman. No qualities are mentioned. The metamessages behind *womanly* call up the home, the hearth, cooking, nurturing.

But surely all of history has shown that women too are strong, brave, courageous. Along with full equality, women will achieve the right to be thought of as energetic, vigorous, and strong—all the qualities we hear behind *manly*—and then the very word *womanly* will undergo a change in our minds.

10

Filling Dead Air

THE NEED TO TALK

In line at the supermarket, an old woman unloads her basket with uncertain hands and smiles tentatively at the checkout clerk. "I haven't been out of the house all week. This weather is awful."

The clerk rings up her items and, in a friendly voice, says, "You look good today."

"Oh, well, my arthritis is better. Besides, walking downstairs is nothing. But going up those steps . . ." Her groceries are checked and bagged, but she lingers a bit. "And how are you today?"

"Not bad. So you're getting two chickens this week. Expecting company?"

"I did hope my sister would make it. She lives out on the island, but with this weather . . ."

"Well, you take care now."

She smiles apologetically at the man behind her, but he pushes his packages forward, and with a final sigh she picks up her bag and leaves.

The clerk, looking after her, shakes his head. The impatient customer says, "All right. Let's get going. I'm on my lunch break."

Still smiling, the clerk says, "Poor old lady. She lives alone, you know, and she has to talk. She buys a few things at a time just as an excuse to come in and chat."

The wistfulness of the old lady, her almost desperate need to speak to someone, anyone, to make some contact with the world outside of her apartment was so strong that it almost pained me to watch. Can anyone live without talking, without simple, everyday conversation, and still enjoy life? Is the need to communicate so great that, deprived of it, we would just waste away?

Even those who seal themselves off from the world, the recluses and hermits, talk to their pets or to themselves. And some, when only a minimum of conversation is available, take what they can from the television set. Sometimes they are even driven to answer back the people on the screen. Still others, like the old woman at the supermarket, are compelled to leave their home to seek out anyone who will listen to them or talk to them.

A friend of ours told us of his encounter with a lonely old man. Tim seems to always invite confidences. "I was walking through the park with a book," he recalled, "looking for a place to sit and read. The only empty bench had an old man sitting at one end of it, his body turned toward the middle of the bench, one arm along the top.

"It was the only place to sit, and I eased myself down, knowing I was trapped. I had to return his smile. His very posture included me in an intimate circle.

"Once I smiled, he bent forward. 'It's a nice day,

isn't it?' It was a standard opening. I could always nod, turn my back, and open my book . . . but I felt sorry for him.

" 'Yes, it is,' I said, smiling. 'It's about time the weather changed.'

"It was what he was waiting for. He moved a few inches closer. 'I come here every day, rain or shine. I'm retired now . . .' and with a sigh I put my book away. I was touched by his need to talk, his desire to communicate."

The overwhelming need to talk that disarmed our friend must be the most important difference between man and animal. It seems that part of the human condition is to converse, to speak and to listen, and, in listening, to shape further speech, to reply to and absorb another's thoughts as you express your own.

And yet there is more to our conversational need than the exchange of thoughts. There is an exchange on the metalevel that is almost as satisfying, almost as necessary.

Tim also told us of another conversational encounter. "It was a park bench again," he laughed. "I was in Paris, an American who couldn't speak French, sitting on a bench in the Tuileries studying my Michelin guide. A young Algerian man sat down next to me, smiled, and asked me a question. I spread my hands to signal incomprehension and used my limited French to say, *'Je ne parle pas le francais.'*

"With an understanding nod and a *'Oui, oui!'* he launched into an animated conversation. For half an hour we sat and talked, I in English and he in French.

"We parted friends, each of us realizing that on a language level we understood little of what the other was saying—but there had been communication."

The communication Tim meant was the metalanguage behind the words that he and the Algerian used, the warmth, the humor, the open feelings. These, together with their body language, had said enough to satisfy each and leave each with a friendly feeling. In this conversation, although the words were meaningless, Tim felt a world of meaning in the signals behind the words.

RITUALS AND CUES

You meet an acquaintance on a city street, and exchange a brief bit of talk. *How are you? Fine. Great weather. What's new? Nothing much. See you soon. Have a happy.* The phrases fall from your lips effortlessly, and they seem to have no meaning. It is a ritual we all go through. However, the ritual can be broken. Someone asks, "How are *you?*" and you hear a metasignal of genuine concern in his voice and pick up the way he stresses *you,* and you realize that he is asking for more than a ritual answer.

But even this concern can be answered with a ritual. We had an aunt who recently died of cancer. While we were visiting her at her worst period, another friend dropped in and, in an anxious voice, asked, "How are *you?*"

Our aunt answered, "Fine," choosing to ignore the metasignals of concern and anxiety. The friend understood that she didn't want to talk about her condition and accepted her meaningless *fine,* then went on to some other matter.

Most of us abide by the ritual, and usually we are not even aware of what we are saying when we engage in this kind of conversation. We ask, "How are you?" but we would feel put upon if the other person really told us just how she was instead of giving the ritual answer. Yet, as meaningless as the rituals seem, the metasignals behind them send out important messages.

"How are you?" signals *I recognize you and I greet you.*

"Fine" signals *I return your recognition and greeting.*

And the same type of message applies to *How're things? How's tricks? What's new? Have a nice day,* and all the others. They are all meaningless, but necessary, rituals of conversation. To bypass them or to try to break out of them can be troubling. If you don't believe it, try to break the rules sometimes. Answer "How are you?" with "Do you mean physically or mentally?"

The answer will usually draw a startled response, followed by annoyance masked with a laugh. And yet it seems a valid conversational ploy. The problem is, it breaks the ritual. Or try answering the same question with a detailed description of just how you do feel and watch the grim veil of boredom descend over the questioner.

Much of the humor of the old Marx Brothers' routines was based on the literal acceptance of some of these rituals. A saleswoman would ask Groucho, "Can I help you?" and he would leer at her and say, "What did you have in mind?"

The refusal to accept the ritual brought on a startled reaction. It was acting, of course, but it reflected the real-life code. You do not fool around with ritual. It serves an important function, as an ice-breaker, a comfort, a gesture of friendship or recognition, or a sign of caring. The metamessages speak behind the words and say all these things and more.

Once the rituals are over, if there is to be real conversation, an exchange of ideas and knowledge, there are still certain rules we must follow, certain signals and cues, on a metacommunicative level that will guide the conversation along. The most important of these are the terminal signals, those metamessages that tell us when a speaker is finished and when it is our turn to speak. Without an understanding of these cues, conversation can become chaos.

Unfortunately, there are many people who either choose to ignore these metacues, or else have never learned to use them. Talking to such people can be a confusing and sometimes harrowing experience. They falter and stumble midway through a sentence. They go on endlessly, and we either interrupt them in the wrong place, or we fail to interrupt them in the right place. When we begin to talk, they interrupt us, or when we give them the right termination cue they don't seem to realize that it is their turn to speak.

In the motion picture *Annie Hall,* Diane Keaton based a good deal of Annie's character on this confusion about metacues. She stumbled and fumbled with words and sentences. She became confused and rattled as she sent out contradictory messages. Keaton's skillful acting tied all the confusion into charm, but in real life the result of such a mishmash is usually far from charming. We're more likely to be driven to distraction by verbal Annie Halls.

What are the terminal cues? There are three very simple ones. When we ask a question we raise our voices. "Is it raining outside?" The voice goes up at the end, at *side*. For a statement, the voice drops at the last syllable. "It's just a drizzle." Down on *zle*. And when you haven't finished a statement, when you mean to keep talking, you signal that too. The voice remains level, neither rising nor falling. The metamessage is *I have something else to say*.

Every once in a while we hear a public speaker

(President Carter is an example) who hasn't sorted out the terminal cues. These speakers keep their voices level as they finish a statement, and we are left waiting to hear more, but that's all there is. Or their voices will rise when they are not asking a question. Without quite knowing why, we react, at first with confusion and then with annoyance, to the misplaced signals.

FEEDBACK, PAUSE FILLERS, AND DISCLAIMERS

Another extremely important element in conversation is feedback. Without positive or negative feedback we have no way of knowing whether we are boring or charming our conversational partner. There are few things as disturbing as talking to someone who sends out no feedback. After a few moments you realize that you are getting no clues to your partner's agreement or disagreement. Is he with you, against you, or lost completely? The emotional impact can be embarrassing and even devastating. It can signal disagreement, hostility, disbelief, or total boredom.

The feedback cues are very simple, and most of us use them without thinking. While researching this book, one of us visited the University of Kansas to talk to a professor in the Linguistics Department, tape recording the entire interview.

When we sat down later with the tapes, we were amazed at the number of Yeahs, Uhuhs, and Yesses that we used constantly while the man we were interviewing talked. They sounded superfluous on tape, but in conversation they were very necessary. They signaled, in metalanguage, *I understand you. You're telling me what I want to hear. You're on the right track*

Sometimes they said, *I'm ahead of you. I want you to hurry through this because I know it* or, occasionally, *I'm bored with this!*

In conversation, the use of Yeah, or any other feedback signal, says, for the most part, *I agree with you.* It serves to encourage your partner to keep talking. It lets him know you are interested, you agree, you want more.

More and more, in today's communicative world, no conversation seems complete without a sprinkling of pause fillers. An athlete will tell an interviewer on television, "I like running, you know. It's healthy and it gets me, you know, out in the open, where I can, you know, get the fresh air I need."

Sometimes it goes beyond a sprinkling. A popular radio station that specializes in talk shows computed just how much time was wasted with *uh, rr, you know, I mean, see, like, know what I mean?* and a few others and came up with close to one third of air time.

At this station, pause fillers are now forbidden to announcers and talk-show hosts, but there's little they can do about their guests.

Pause fillers are those little phrases we throw into any conversation at no logical interval, and, according to most psycholinguists, we use them to fill the awkward moments when we are gathering our thoughts together. Unfortunately, they vry soon become habitual, and hardly a sentence comes out without them.

There is rarely any metamessage intended by the person using a pause filler. It is an automatic response. But a metamessage does come across to the listener, particularly when he doesn't use pause fillers himself. The message is usually one of irritation and impatience. Someone is taking too long to get his message across, or else he doesn't know what he wants to say.

Pause fillers are negative signals, not necessary to

conversation—indeed they often hinder communication. But still, to many of us, they seem necessary. Is it that we are afraid of a slight pause, of silence? Do we feel that if we stop to gather our thoughts together our conversational partner will jump in and take over? Or is it that we often speak too soon, before we know what we want to say, and the pause llers slow us down?

Another negative element in conversation is the disclaimer. This can be a self-deprecating little laugh at the end of a sentence, a laugh that seems to deny what has just been said. Its metasignal says, *I'm uncertain. I'm insecure. I'm vulnerable. I didn't really mean it. Feel free to attack me.*

The disclaimer can be a phrase, usually tacked on after a slightly challenging or daring remark. *I guess. I think.* Or *Wasn't it?* "It was an awful movie—wasn't it?" "We should make a right turn here—I think." "It's a very nice place for a vacation—I guess." Each disclaimer apologizes for the speaker's temerity in daring to make a positive statement. The disclaimer also gives the other person a lever with which to disagree.

SILENCE AND THE OVERRIDE

One of the hindrances to full conversation is silence. Renata Adler, in her novel, *Speedboat,* wrote, "There are . . . people who just sit there, silent. A question is addressed to them. They do not answer. Another question, silence. It is a position of great power. Talkative people, running toward these silences, are jarred, time after time, by a straight-arm rebuff."

In that sense, silence can be destructive, and, with

no spoken message, still send out an intense negative metasignal. *I will not let you reach me!* Every parent has come up against the silence of a child who does not wish to listen or be convinced. In metacommunication, the silence screams out, *I will not listen! I will not hear you!*

Only a few generations ago we accepted the fact that children should be seen and not heard. Nowadays we ask them with some despair, "Why don't you talk?" We beg for communication. But we should remember that with children silence can signal a retreat from hurt Children who were victims of verbal assault will often retreat into silence. Their metamessage is *I will not allow the hurt to get through my protective wall of silence*

A husband who talked to us of his marital problems said, "When my wife pulls that number on me, that silence routine, I'm completely defeated. There's nothing worse than someone who won't argue, who won't discuss what's wrong. I can fight anything, but not that. When she's silent, she's withdrawn, miles away and I just can't reach her."

But as negative as silence can be in a conversation, it can also, under certain circumstances, be a positive device The sympathetic silence, the understanding silence, the listening silence are all strong devices to help a conversation along and weld the talkers closer together

In the use of silence, timing is all important. You must know just when to talk and when to be silent Silence, at an inappropriate time, becomes the power play Adler wrote of. At an appropriate time, it becomes an encouraging strength

Timing is just as essential in other elements of conversation We pick up a partner's metasignals when she is talking to us, and if we pick them up at just the right time the conversation plunges ahead. But wait too long to pick up the cues, wait too long when someone signals that it's your turn to speak, and the entire structure of the conversation can be spoiled. You miss the rhythm and it becomes impossible to recover it.

But at the other extreme, pick up the cues too quickly, answer the question before it's asked, and you frustrate your partner. She never gets a chance to finish her sentence and her train of thought is jarred.

There is another disadvantage to missing cues in conversation, to waiting too long to pick them up or answering too quickly. We have all talked to bores or listened to people who dragged on beyond the point of interest while we searched desperately for some way to turn them off.

There is a point at which a bore can be cut off without sending hostile metasignals. But let him go beyond that point, let him talk just a bit too long, and you are trapped, caught up in his conversation, and there is no way out without being rude.

Along with bores, there are those people who dominate a conversation by overriding the other. They deliberately refuse to give the cues that will allow you to interrupt them. They keep a level tone all through their talk and never send the up or down message that says, *I'm finished. Now it's your turn.*

Without receiving these signals, you can only get your turn by interrupting the other's speech. This is an aggressive act, and many of us feel reluctant to take it. This is particularly true of women. They are accustomed to having men override them, and rather than break in, many will retreat with a defensive smile, or simply "turn off."

There are, of course, many women who use the override to dominate the conversation themselves. The henpecked husband who can't get a word in is a popular stereotype, and there are many men like him, but on an overall count, most men are ahead of women in this trick.

THE METAPERSONA GAME

Whenever we talk we send out a complicated variety of metasignals, and with each person we talk to we use a different set of signals. In a sense, we assume a different persona for each. Sometimes it is an authoritative persona, sometimes a submissive one. The same person, in different surroundings, can change to an angry persona, a loving one, a teaching one, a learning one, or any one of hundreds of others Which persona we assume depends on the situation and our relationship to the people we are involved with

Take Betty and Don, two guests at a small dinner party with some friends and neighbors. Listening in on some of the conversations will tell us what persona each person assumes.

Betty tells her neighbor Merril, "My Jill is so stimulated by the Intellectually Gifted Children's class at school "

Merril answers with an uninterested, "Is she really?" But her lack of interest is defensive She senses what's coming.

"It's a shame," Betty goes on, "that a bright boy like your Billy isn't in the IGC class." There is genuine sympathy in Betty's voice and she can afford it because her metamessage is not in how the words are said, but in the words themselves, and Merril knows exactly what that metamessage is. *Billy is not Jill's equal intellectually*. Betty has assumed her superior persona

To most people, Betty presents a compassionate persona, but Merril rubs her the wrong way, and this is a chance to get some of her own back. Yet, if you were to challenge Betty, she wouldn't be aware of the destructive metasignals her words send out. She's convinced herself that she's genuinely interested in Billy.

As the evening goes on, Betty talks to many people, and for each one she assumes a different persona. When she is introduced to Dr. Richard Talbert and his wife, Corinne, Betty assumes two different personas, one for the doctor and the other for his wife.

"Dr. Talbert, you're new in this area, and I'm so happy to meet you." This one is enthusiasm, with deference and flattery. "I've heard so much about you."

When she turns her attention to the doctor's wife, the pitch, tone, even the rhythm of her voice changes, along with her persona. There is enthusiasm, but neither deference nor flattery. "We're all so glad to have an internist in the neighborhood, Corinne." The use of the first name implies an intimacy that she could not presume with Corinne's husband, the doctor. With him, it's Dr. Talbert, a form of flattery that most of us use toward someone of higher status.

Most of the men and women at the party will follow Betty's example and address the husband as Dr. Talbert, the wife as Corinne. The one exception is Judge Levy. As the evening wears on, he'll drop the doctor and begin to call him Richard. He might even go so far as the familiar Dick. His persona is equality.

Dr. Talbert, though he addresses everyone else by his first name, will continue to call Judge Levy Judge, and we can see he's assumed the same persona of deference that Betty assumed when she spoke to him. Judge Levy is higher in status than Dr. Talbert.

Let's do a little more eavesdropping. Betty's husband, Don, is seated next to Roger. Both men are in the real-estate business.

"How's it going?" Roger asks. "Business good?"

"Not bad, I sold that big tract over by the high school to a group of investors," Don answers casually. But Roger notices the tone of self-satisfaction. *Not every broker could pull off a deal like that.*

Roger slips into his own persona of bigger shot and says, "Yeah. I know that property. We were handling it for a while, but I turned it over to one of the kids in the office when I took off last month."

Roger has scored a hole-in-one in the Metapersona Game. A property deal like Don's is kid stuff, and what's more, he can take a month off in this busy season.

Don, out of his depth, says, "You've been away?"

Wrong play to Roger. With his exclusive act, Roger says, "Had to get some sun. Had a hell of a season."

"I noticed the tan. Miami?"

Roger raises his voice a bit. "Miami? God, no! We found this little town on the Pacific coast of Mexico. Not a tourist in sight. Some South American millionaires with their yachts and a few Hollywood people—what was the name of that TV director, dear?" he asks his wife.

"Don't tell anyone the name of the town," his wife warns, "or in a few years it will be just like Acapulco!"

The two of them wear their exclusive metapersonas with flair, but they aren't all that unusual. Name dropping, place dropping, phrase dropping are all signals of the exclusive routine. Roger casually drops a few more names of people who found his "little town in Mexico." Someone else drops the name of a charming little island in the Caribbean. "Saba has no beach, you know, but the fantastic villages hanging on the sides of the mountain . . ." And that reminds another guest of a "primitive little spot in Yugoslavia . . ."

This is all getting out of hand. Not many of the guests can afford Europe, so Betty brings the name dropping back home to a "darling little restaurant on the other side of town," and adds, "No one's found it yet."

People and places are good for name dropping, but things can do as well. "This wine is good, but we discovered this fantastic '76 Beaujolais . . ." or else, "I got the pâté at a little shop run by two boys. They keep it for their special customers," and so it goes.

In all these little ploys and gambits, the metasignals around the words are secondary. The words themselves hold the metamessage, *that little shop, that darling island, that heavenly dressmaker*—it's all in the way you carry your persona of exclusiveness.

Sometimes the introduction is important. "You mean you've never heard of . . .?" This can be any person, place, or thing, a book, a play, a film, a poem. Another favorite approach is "Of course you've seen Spalvanie's new film." This gambit puts you on the spot. Do you dare admit you've never heard of Spalvanie? The flattery can be broader. "I was sure someone like you would know Glockenspiel's hidden symphony."

Finally, the use of foreign or obscure phrases in ordinary conversation rounds out the exclusive persona. The foreign phrase can be as simple as "The book has an air of *je ne sais quoi*" or as vague as "Politics? Oh well, *plus ça change, plus c'est la même chose*" or, if you like a classical touch, "So they finally got together. Well, I always say, *Fata viam invenient. . . .*"

With any of these, you must remember, pronunciation is all important. You're probably safer with French than with Latin. The safest, of course, is a quote so obscure that no one has heard it before.

A TRULY HUMAN GAME

Is it necessary to try on all these different personas and play these games? In certain social circles, everyone assumes a persona and you assume one at your own risk. Admittedly, sometimes it is fun to throw around a bit of knowledge, to bolster your own ego and even put someone else down. Part of being human is to lie, exaggerate, and even to hurt, but remember, a little knowledge can be a dangerous thing. You must always keep in mind that this sort of communication sends out a metamessage of superficiality, and it can cut off any real conversation. By being glib and surfacy, you can miss out on the pleasure of true and deep intimacy.

In conversation, as in any intimate relationship, we should share and exchange parts of our self, our knowledge, our thoughts, and our emotions. We also share each other's personality. If we reveal only the self we think others will find acceptable and hide behind the metasignals of put-downs and one-upmanship, we will cut off any chances of honest friendship. Sharing a wonderful vacation on an undiscovered beach in Mexico can be done by simply telling about it without the destructive game playing.

Another metagame that we often play on a conversational level is the professional, or job, gambit. The teacher who teaches when he talks, the psychiatrist who analyzes, the minister who pontificates are all guilty of this. Often it is not so much what they say as the way they say it.

We can remember a literary cocktail party where, as we moved from group to group, people's professions were revealed by their metacommunication. In one corner a minister was discussing a new movie, and, while he never mentioned religion, each phrase was delivered in rolling, sonorous tones. By the bar, a sociologist was arguing with a writer, her words matching her metasignals. "I don't think you've fully explored the internal reasons behind poverty and unemployment. . . ."

There were a politician politicizing, a lawyer trying every subject, a doctor diagnosing, and rich men, poor men, beggar men, and thieves, all carrying over their professional metacommunication into their social life.

Even Lonnie, a stand-up comic in from the Coast, played the game by the same rules. Before his coat was off, his mouth was working. "The funniest story of the week. This will kill you. . . ." He gets his laugh and before anyone can answer he has another story.

Lonnie is funny, and he dominates every party, but after a few minutes he begins to wear. He hasn't learned the prime rule in talking to one person or a group—give the other a chance to talk.

ARE YOU LISTENING?

If someone speaks and no one listens, can there be a conversation? Dr. S. I. Hayakawa, the noted linguist, once wrote, ". . . few people other than psychiatrists and women have had much training in listening." And yet listening should be an integral part of any conversation. Without it talk flows at random. There is no real communication, no transfer of ideas and concepts. The inclination to boost our own ego often deafens us to our partner's words. We become so involved with what *we* want to say next that we neglect to listen to *him* at all.

Listening is a skill in itself, and metalistening is an important aspect of that skill. If we are sensitive listeners, we pick up and assimilate all the metasignals that are sent along with the words, and we quickly decide if they are compatible with the words.

Unfortunately, most of us are defensive listeners, too busy readying our own replies to give our full attention to what is being said. Because of this we often miss not only the literal message but all the metasignals behind it.

Let's eavesdrop on a family when Dad comes home, hot and tired from a long train ride, to find an equally hot and tired Mom.

DAD: Hey, what's for dinner? It's after seven.

MOM: I've had a terrible day. Johnny scraped his leg in the playground, and I never got to the market to shop. I just feel rotten!

DAD: Come on, what kind of a day do you think I had? I'm starving. Is it too much to ask for a decent meal when I get home?

MOM: What do you want me to do? I just haven't had a chance to get out of the house.

DAD: Well, that's your problem. My problem is, I'm hungry, and I think I've a right to come home and find a meal on the table!

He storms out of the room and Mom dissolves in tears.

Admittedly, this father is a bit of an autocrat, even if he's had a rough day. Mom had a rough one too, overwhelmed by the kids and house. Still, both of them are insensitive listeners. They hear only the words in each other's communications. True, they each have legitimate complaints, but if either had decided to try metalistening, there would have been a different ending to the unpleasant and frustrating conversation.

Let's run the scenario through again with one partner using metalistening. Let Mom be the wise one since Hayakawa thinks women are better at listening.

DAD: Hey, what's for dinner? It's after seven.

MOM: You sound starved and exhausted. Was the commuting rough?

DAD: It sure was. Man, I could eat a cow.

MOM: No cows around. Sit down and unwind while I fix something. The kids are watching TV. Should I get you a drink? It sounds as if you had a hard day.

DAD: Have I ever! Forget the drink. I'll set the table and talk to you while you get dinner.

Here Mom has picked up the metasignals of tiredness and frustration in her husband's voice. In turn, she offers a soothing murmur of sympathy. Instead of airing her own complaints now, she listens to his and tries to understand how he feels. She may have to wait to get her problems out, but that can come later. She has put herself in his place and has tried to empathize with him.

The husband, in this same situation, could also have tried the metalistening approach. Let's play the scenario that way and see how it runs.

DAD: Hey, what's for dinner? It's after seven.

MOM: I've had a terrible day. Johnny scraped his leg in the playground and I never got to the market to shop. I just feel rotten.

DAD: You feel lousy, huh?
MOM: You better believe it!
DAD: And nothing went right. One of those days.
MOM: You put your finger on it. I don't know what to do for dinner.
DAD: Look, I'll mix us a drink while you open a can of something.
MOM: I could make a nice crabmeat salad. I have some leftovers in the fridge. . . .

Here the husband used metalistening to sense theexhaustion in his wife's voice. His sympathy and understanding lets her know that he appreciates what she does and knows how hard it is to take care of the kids and house. He wants to make things easier.

The trick here, as in all metalistening, is not to respond to the words alone. In this case the feelings of exhaustion and frustration have as strong an emotional impact as the actual words. In another situation, the metamessage might be sadness, guilt, vulnerability, or even joy. Any one of hundreds of emotions can be sent out. What the listener must be aware of is *every part* of the communication. He must listen and actually hear the metacues, then understand and assimilate them before he answers.

Carl Rogers, of California's Center for Studies of the Person, in his writing on active listening gives us clues that can be easily applied to metalistening. A point he makes is that when people are listened to sensitively, they tend to listen with more sensitivity themselves. Take this example. At a social gathering, one man tells another, "I've just seen the most incredible SciFi movie. You wouldn't believe the special effects!"

The other hears special effects and immediately comes up with a competitive reaction. "Special effects? Have you seen *Star Wars?* Now *there* were special effects. Those fantastic ships . . ."

Not to be outdone, the first says, "But those were big-scale. I saw this one scene . . ." And it goes on like that, each interested in describing his own reaction, each waiting for the other to finish but not listening to what he says, just concentrating on what to answer.

This is the very opposite of metalistening. It becomes a conversation where each speaker is locked into his own private world. Instead of listening to the other, each waits for the other to finish only so he can speak himself.

In metalistening, you listen on two levels. While the other is speaking you hear not only the words but also the emotions behind them, and then you attempt to sum up what has been said—but in a different way. It is important to let the speaker know that you've really heard him before you contribute your own thoughts to the conversation. One of the easiest ways to do this is to rephrase part of what he says.

A woman tells her friend, "I'm annoyed at the way Peter acted at the party last night." If her friend is metalistening, she'll answer, "You feel angry with him." The friend is not agreeing with her about Peter's actions. She's just letting her know that she heard her words and the anger behind them.

This type of approach can do a great deal toward letting the other person understand and explore her own anger Susan is an example of this. The way her mother treats her breaks through the barrier of her anger. She comes home from school and throws her books down on the kitchen table. "Mrs. Shelton gave me a C on my term paper. It just isn't fair!"

Her mother hears all of Susan's message, not only the anger but the disappointment behind the words.

"You feel she wasn't fair." She uses the word feel to let her daughter know that she understands how disappointed she is.

"I worked so hard, Mom!"

"I know you did. Why, you stayed up till one o'clock last Monday." Mother still has not passed judgment or said what she feels about Susan's low mark. Instead she has shown empathy for her daughter's problem. Putting herself in Susan's shoes, she realizes how terrible it must be to get a C in the course.

But Susan picks up what her mother has said. "Maybe I shouldn't have waited till Monday night to do the paper. Mrs. Shelton is such a hard marker."

Now mother can reveal some of her own thoughts on the subject. "You always say you learn more in her class than any other. Maybe she expects more of you."

"She sure does." Susan sounds less angry.

"Do you think she might let you redo the paper?"

"Gee, I might ask her. It's worth a try. Thanks, Mom."

Susan's mother is not only an active metalistener, she is a sensitive one. She could have handled it the way most parents do, blamed Susan for the low mark, refused to listen to her excuses, and, in the long run, aggravated the problem. By metalistening, she was able to let Susan work out her problem to some extent and explore her feelings about her own work. When a solution seemed possible, Susan was ready to accept it.

It's not an easy job, metalistening. We all tend to evaluate what someone says instead of understanding the emotions behind their statement. Someone tells us something and we immediately judge it, disagree or agree and then categorize the speaker. Take this conversation between two men at a bar.

"The women in this country are getting out of hand. They want everything."

Hearing this, you can either agree, "You're right," or disagree, "That's nonsense!" or categorize the speaker "You know, you're a male-chauvinist pig!"

But if you metalistened, you might hear through his words and try to understand why he felt what he did. Perhaps he was influenced by the bitterness of a personal experience. The trick is to put yourself in his place, realize why he feels so strongly, and then restate what he has said to show him that you are listening. "You feel that women are getting more than men."

"God, yes! My son was on the waiting list at a top medical school, and they passed right over him to give the place to a girl."

"Your son was passed over because they wanted a woman."

If you listen carefully to his words, you'll hear the metasignals of anger and bitterness, but now they seem less violent. He lowers his voice. "I'm not against women having equal rights, but in this case my son should have gotten in."

Now you are ready to explore what has happened, and, as his anger simmers down, you can allow some of your own feelings on the subject to surface. Even if the discussion ends in disagreement, it is important that at no point should you become so involved in your defense, or so angry at his viewpoint, that you stop listening.

It's not an easy or a simple process, and it carries a certain risk with it. The danger is that once you succeed in putting yourself in his place, you risk having your own feelings and opinions changed. But that's what conversation is all about. It is not only revealing your own thoughts and feelings, but learning the thoughts and feelings of others.

Conversation, in many ways, is the acknowledgment of being, of your being and your partner's being, and this, perhaps, is behind our drive to converse and communicate. It is, after all, a drive to acknowledge ourselves.

11

Coming In Loud and Clear

A recent article in a national news magazine reported on a group of researchers investigating the various methods that officials have used in dealing with terrorists and desperate men who held hostages. After dozens of interviews, they concluded that the most important factor in handling such a situation successfully and getting the hostages away unharmed was for the lawmen involved to get to know the enemy. Listen to him, they advised, and understand what lies behind his desperation. Tune in on that other wavelength beyond his words.

We can interpret what they are saying to mean "Understand his metacommunication and use it to select your own words and your own metasignals in order to manipulate the situation to your own advantage." His metamessages will tell you how to respond, when to show sympathy and understanding, when to move in on him, when he is at the point of exhaustion, when he is ready to blow up, or when he is no longer dangerous.

A policeman we interviewed told us of an incident when he spent hours trying to talk a young woman out of jumping from the ledge of a high-rise apartment house. "It was when she began to talk about her children that I realized I had made a breakthrough. Her words were jumbled together and often she didn't seem to be making sense, but I could hear a desperate note of concern in her voice. I was honestly able to say, 'You really love those kids!' I felt for her. I sensed, from something in her voice, that she was a woman driven by despair."

After he had picked up that despairing metasignal behind her words, he was able to add understanding and sympathy to his own voice. Up until that moment, there had been only talking between them. Now he was able to dig below the surface and feed her the emotional support she needed. By using the right metacues he became her ally. An hour later she took his outstretched hand and allowed him to pull her back from the ledge.

Not many of us are involved in situations as dramatic as this, but all of us have experienced moments of great stress when words seem to fail or become meaningless. At times like this, metacommunication can still send out love, grief, sadness, hate, anger, joy, and all the other emotions a human is capable of feeling.

Jules Henry, the sociologist, in his book *Culture against Man,* says that if, in every human contact, "something is communicated, something learned and something felt, it follows that when nothing is communicated, learned and felt, there is nothing human either."

He could have added that where there is no metacommunication, there is also nothing human. Metacommunication is the wellspring of humanity. No matter what we say, in the end what is of importance is the way we say it.

The parent who tells her child "I love you" with no conviction, with no metasignals of love behind the words, might just as well say, *I have no feeling for you*. The wife who tells her husband "I believe in you" must strengthen her words with metalanguage; otherwise, there is no belief, no conviction to her statement.

All of us, in whatever situation, association, or relationship we find ourselves, must back up our words with the signals and cues of metalanguage or else we communicate in a mechanical and inhuman way.

In modern times, radio and television, relayed by satellites, can let us know what is being said on the other side of the world at the very moment it is happening. The voices and faces of famous people have become familiar to all of us, and the entire earth has shrunk to the distance between us and our TV sets.

The techniques of communication have become so perfected and so widespread that our President can talk to the majority of citizens before, during, and after any national emergency. Yet, while all this goes on, on a personal level more and more people complain, "Nobody really communicates anymore."

What is really lacking in this explosion of communication is an awareness of how we talk to one another. Perhaps, like the lawman and the terrorist or the policeman and the potential suicide, we must begin to listen for that other wavelength behind the words, and at the same time allow our emotional signals to surface. Learning to do this will give an added dimension to our speech, even while we become aware of the added dimension in the speech of others.

Because metacommunication is emotional rather than intellectual, much, if not all of it, is unconscious. Consciously, you may select the words you use, but how you deliver those words, the emotional packaging you use, is the way you tell your listener what you feel about him, about the message, and about yourself.

Usually you are unaware of the different and complicated metawavelengths you use, but you can learn ways of controlling them by opening your ears and your mind to all the hidden signals, the emotional tipoffs, the unconscious messages behind the words. Only then can you move from the unconscious to the conscious, and in doing so become aware of what you say, how you say it, and why you say it—on the metalevel

Such awareness is the first step in mastering metacommunication, but it can also be a stumbling block. Too much deliberation, too much selection of just the right tone of voice, too much concentration on volume, speed, and inflection will make your speech artificial and awkward.

If you use all that you have learned in this book in a conscious effort to manipulate people, you may succeed, but you may also run into trouble. There is a moral issue involved here. We know that actors, politicians, and salesmen are experts at such verbal manipulation, and in a sense we expect it of them. It's one of the techniques they use to make their living.

But what about the rest of us, Mr. and Ms. Ordinary Citizen? What happens when we use the same science as a way of manipulating others in everyday life? Is it good or bad to try to influence lovers, parents, mates, children, friends, and business acquaintances? Is there a set of standards we can apply to such verbal maneuvering? Is there positive manipulation as well as negative?

In a broad sense, there are both kinds. Attempting to manipulate others for power, as in a put-down, to increase your own ego, as in emotional blackmail, or in any other selfish or destructive way will open all the negative aspects of metacommunication.

However, if there is honesty behind the words and behind your use of the metabands, then there is no doubt that you will improve communication, open yourself and your listener to a greater understanding or intimacy, and get your message across clearer and more precisely. You will, in effect, be coming in loud and clear on the metaband!

In the course of writing this book, we found that we too began to listen, not only to what people were saying but also to how they were saying it, to the metasignals and metamessages behind their words. At first it was awkward and uncomfortable. That extra listening seemed to get in the way of ordinary conversation. Sometimes, in fact, we read more into what someone was saying than was really meant. But that changed very quickly, and a new sensitivity, an honesty in trying to understand others became an almost automatic process.

In the same way we learned to hear our own voices, to hear with that same sensitive ear what and how we were communicating.

Once you start listening to how you speak, you are forced to examine how much honesty or pretense exists in your communication, and you also realize how much of yourself you are willing to reveal in every encounter.

Perhaps, in a sense, what we are all asking for is to be recognized and understood, and the only way we can convey this basic human need is through words and emotions, the fabric of communication and metacommunication.